THE BIG RELIEF

THE BIG RELIEF

the urgency of grace for a worn-out world

DAVID ZAHL

BrazosPress
a division of Baker Publishing Group
Grand Rapids, Michigan

Published by Brazos Press
a division of Baker Publishing Group
Grand Rapids, Michigan
BrazosPress.com

Printed in the United States of America

Library of Congress Cataloging-in-Publication Data
Names: Zahl, David, 1979– author.
Title: The big relief : the urgency of grace for a worn-out world / David Zahl.
Description: Grand Rapids, Michigan : Brazos Press, a division of Baker Publishing Group,
    [2025] | Includes bibliographical references.
Identifiers: LCCN 2024038275 | ISBN 9781587435577 (cloth) | ISBN 9781493449620 (ebook)
Subjects: LCSH: Grace (Theology)
Classification: LCC BT761.3 .Z33 2025 | DDC 234—dc23/eng/20240926
LC record available at https://lccn.loc.gov/2024038275

The names and details of the people and situations described in this book have been changed or presented in composite form in order to ensure the privacy of those with whom the author has worked.

Cover design by Chris Kuhatschek

Published in association with The Bindery Agency, www.TheBinderyAgency.com.

25 26 27 28 29 30 31   7 6 5 4 3 2 1

For John and Simeon

Nothing else in the world matters
but the kindness of grace,
God's gift to suffering mortals.

—*Jack Kerouac,*
journal entry

CONTENTS

ACKNOWLEDGMENTS

Deepest thanks to my editor, Katelyn Beaty, for lending such generous attention and sharp instincts to every aspect of this project. To my agent, Alex Field, for shepherding it in the first place.

To my treasured colleagues at Christ Church Charlottesville—Paul Walker, Josh Bascom, Amanda McMillen, and Sam Bush—who encouraged me every step of the way and covered when I needed extra writing time. To the Mockingboard—Jonathan Adams, Ginger Mayfield, Scott Johnson, Jim Munroe, Emily Large, Michael Sansbury, and Reid Murchison—for their tireless support and cheerleading. To my dear friends and cohosts on the *Mockingcast*, Sarah Condon and R. J. Heijmen, with whom I had the privilege of exploring much of this material initially, for never letting me take myself too seriously. To my brothers in F3Cville, not just for the bearcrawl and mumblechatter but for also keeping me in touch with my inner child. For all the other heaven-sent helpers who have embodied the Big Relief these past couple years, especially Marilu Thomas, Karen D-J, Claire Hopkins, J. Daemlich, and Paul H.

To the amazing Mockingbird staff—Deanna Roche, Todd Brewer, Meaghan Ritchey, Luke Roland, Cali Yee, and Katie Henson—for keeping the lights on and bearing with me during the months of drafting. To Micah Gilmer, the best citation hound in the biz. To my readers C. J. Green and Will McDavid, whose literary chops astound me and without whom this book would be a shadow of itself.

To my brother John, who remains the most trusted repository of "stories of grace" around and from whom so many of the illustrations herein derive. To my brother Simeon, who's all right too, I guess. (God willing, he knows how much this manuscript relied on his genius to come together.) To my beloved parents, Mary and Paul, who have never crossed their fingers when it comes to the grace of God—not even when it came to their own boys.

And finally, to my wife, Cate, whose love keeps me sane, whose jokes keep me laughing, and whose recommendations keep me inspired. Without her brilliance and sacrifice this book would not exist.

INTRODUCTION

"Don't feel bad. We *have* to have a place we can vent," my coworker said. We had just signed off of a frustrating conference call and, per our custom, had spent the next fifteen minutes "debriefing." This was code for complaining and psychoanalyzing. Clearly, we were both feeling self-conscious about this ritual of ours.

The day was almost over, but I was worked up, so I decided to stop by the gym on the way home to blow off a little steam. Half an hour on the treadmill always does wonders for my mood, provided, of course, that the music in my AirPods is blasting loud enough to drown out any noise from the TVs, which are always tuned to cable news.

The postexercise glow felt great, but it was fleeting. Once I walked in the door at home, the kids were on top of me, competing to report about their days, asking for homework help, petitioning for more dessert, more screen time, more attention than any well-meaning father can muster. Happy as I was to see them, the chaotic clambering didn't stop until 10:00 p.m. and the last of their lights went out.

Of course, my wife had been dealing with their insanity all afternoon, and the look with which she greeted me said it all. She was off duty, ready for a bath and some Hulu. She'd be ready to reengage in a couple hours, but until then I was on my own.

I wondered if maybe the two of us could get out of Dodge soon and refuel a bit before the holiday season began—not that we had any spare cash at the moment, not with what felt like every single bill "adjusting upward" at the same time. Oh well. The kids had games every single weekend for the next few months anyway. Heaven forbid that we skip the tournament where that long-awaited first home run happens.

Some housework had to be done before I hit the sack. Thankfully, I had a decent audiobook to help turn my brain off while folding laundry, a better pre-bed wind-down than perusing social media, right? Some guys would reward themselves with a beer at this point, but I am more apt to treat myself to some late-night Ben & Jerry's. Mmmm, mint chocolate cookie. If only the sugar didn't keep me up—a liability when sleep is the only thing that pauses the anxious chatter within.

I've just described a few hours of the life I know best, that of a fairly comfortable middle-aged husband and father of three. Hopefully, you didn't roll your eyes too hard or make that tiny violin gesture. If you did, I wouldn't blame you. I'm well aware that my outward circumstances register pretty low on the scale of zero to Darfur.

The through line of the day is nevertheless clear. I spent it searching for relief. I don't think I'm alone. *Blowing off steam, venting, zoning out, refueling, winding down, going off-grid, carving out space*—different people use different terms, but they are all euphemisms for the same thing.

We are all chasing relief.

Relief from what exactly? It varies. It could be the drumbeat of demand I describe above—professional, financial, relational. It could be the pressure to succeed or to produce or to be a certain kind of person that our culture esteems, someone with influence and initiative and purpose.

It could be something more mundane that we crave relief from, like the burden of a mortgage payment or the grip of a chronic illness. It could be something larger scale, some form of sociopolitical turmoil that just won't go away. It could be the discouraging and sometimes alarming headlines that greet us every time we look at our phones.

Or it could be something less circumstantial and more existential, like the pressure to justify our lives and demonstrate that we're worthy of the air we breathe. Perhaps it's an internal voice of accusation and not-good-enoughness or the external judgments of others, their biases and prejudices and criticisms. Maybe we long for relief from grief or guilt or the pain of rejection. Some of us, as we'll explore in the following pages, struggle with the pressure to belong, the pressure to keep up, the pressure to say the right thing—the pressure, even, to be our own god, in control of everything.

It could be anything, really. The shape of the pressure fluctuates. Its presence does not.

The experience of being a person is, in many ways, the experience of craving and seeking relief. We want out from under, room to breathe, if just for a little while.

I suspect this drive accounts for a great deal of our endless, and endlessly inventive, attempts to self-medicate—or, in today's parlance, "self-soothe"—which range from the benign to the deadly: beer, chocolate, Netflix, spa days, endorphins, adrenaline, Instagram, OnlyFans, MMORPGs, reality TV, DraftKings, nine holes on the golf course, Zillow, fentanyl. The list could go on and on. We turn to these things for distraction and pleasure, sure, but also for relief. And the truth is, many of them deliver relief of a sort.

But relief is different from—more than—distraction or pleasure. Let's return to the long day I detailed earlier, in which the word *relief* itself was audibly invoked several times. After a check I'd been expecting for months finally arrived in the mail, I described it as a relief. My teenage son came home from school in a non-teenagey mood, which my wife reported as a relief (it very much was). A sick friend called to say he had scored an appointment with a sought-after specialist. He breathed what he called "a big sigh of relief."

In each case, relief refers to the feeling of pressure being removed. This isn't so much a sense of deflation but of removal and respite, like taking off a heavy backpack, tensed muscles being given a break when you sit down. Relief connotes ease.

Of course, relief isn't just affective. When I deposited that check and the funds hit my account, I had something that I didn't have before. The extra cash translated not only to decreased anxiety but also to increased flexibility.

I think of another acquaintance, Robert, whose landlord tried to evict him. The dispute went to court and the judge ruled in Robert's favor, which meant he no longer had to move. Robert was relieved from the pressure of having to do something onerous, to suffer something. Yet it's not just that he'd been spared a stressful upheaval. The time and energy that would have been expended on the madness of the rental market was now his to use however he'd like. Relief, in both instances, rings a note of freedom.

That's not all. When I was in fourth grade, a Category 5 hurricane clobbered the city where I lived. It was a genuine disaster, and now that I'm a parent of similarly aged children, the memory gives me the shivers. We didn't just lose power; we lost water—for almost a week. We got off school for nearly a month while the government coordinated relief efforts. Relief meant money and resources (and lots of chain saws) directed our way. That is, relief took the form of assistance given to those in a desperate situation. I understood the meaning at the time because I was a baseball fanatic. I knew that a relief pitcher comes in at the end of a game to help deliver a victory. Relief has an element of gratuity and deliverance.

Surely people turn to God in search of relief. I know I have and still do. My friend Sarah, who works for a church, likes to wear a shirt emblazoned with the phrase "hope dealer." What is hope if not relief from despair? Jesus himself makes the offer explicit in his invitation, "Come to me, all you who are weary and are carrying heavy burdens, and I will give you rest" (Matt. 11:28). "Lay your burden down," pleads many a gospel singer, and human ears can't help perking up. We are all carrying so much.

4

Yet *relief* is not a word often associated with God today, at least not with the God of Christianity. For a great many folks, G-O-D signifies the opposite of relief. The church, to the extent it enters contemporary thinking at all, is seen (and experienced!) as a purveyor of spiritual and moral burdens, not a place to unload them. It is a place we go to be told what to do rather than to hear about what has been done for us.

Religion, in other words, feels less like a place to seek refuge than a system to seek refuge *from*. Consider the dictionary definition of *sermon*. The *Oxford English Dictionary* defines it as "a discourse (spoken or written) on a serious subject, containing instruction or exhortation. Also contemptuously, a long or tedious discourse or harangue."[1] Does that sound like a relief to you?

Preach, similarly, is defined as "usually derogatory: to give moral or religious advice in a self-righteous, condescending or obtrusive way."[2] No thank you!

These definitions do not describe my personal experience of Christianity. The church has been the place I go when there's no place left to go. The Lord has been a shepherd, not a boss or a disciplinarian but a sure and steady comfort in times of trouble.

Why do some of us experience Christianity as a burden and others as a refuge? The answer, I am convinced, has to do with grace. Grace is the Big Relief at the heart of Christianity. When grace is downplayed or qualified, faith turns into a project and then a burden. Project religion—the ancient human enterprise of proving ourselves morally and spiritually worthy of God's love—is everywhere. You can recognize it by the refugees it drives out.

When anchored to grace, however, Christianity remains good news. More than that, faith becomes a source of energy rather than a drain. Its pastoral and existential heart keeps beating, even in the

---

1. *Oxford English Dictionary*, "sermon," last updated July 2023, https://www.oed.com/dictionary/sermon_n?tab=meaning_and_use.

2. *Oxford English Dictionary*, "preach," last updated March 2024, https://www.oed.com/dictionary/preach_v?tab=meaning_and_use#28787161.

midst of heartache and disillusionment and hurricane-sized disaster. With the grace of God as its foundation, Christianity functions as an engine of love.

You'll note that I've made these claims without really defining what grace is. That's because *grace* is a notoriously elastic word. It means different things to different people in different contexts. The grace of a ballerina is not the same as the grace that families say before dinner. When Roman Catholics use the word, they usually mean something different than Baptists do. Is grace a substance or an inclination? Some days, the only thing we know for sure about grace is that we want more of it—need it, in fact.

Still, I can tell you what *I* mean when I use the word. I'll start with a few favorite slogans. Grace is one-way love. Grace is a gift with no strings attached. It is noncontingent, compassionate alliance. Unmerited favor. Sacrificial love that seeks a person out at their most unlovable.

Theologically speaking, grace is the answer the Bible gives to the question of God's disposition toward troubled people like you and me. This answer is revealed in—and inextricably tied to—the person and work of Jesus Christ. The apostle Paul boiled it down like this: "But God proves his love for us in that while we still were sinners Christ died for us" (Rom. 5:8). Grace is the most evergreen reason that people become Christians, and it is the most compelling reason for remaining one.

To make the connection more explicit, let's return one last time to the day I recounted earlier. In between dinner and the kids' bedtime, there was an important item of business to attend to: the dog. Our terrier, Violet, needed a walk, badly. I knew this because she was clinging to my leg and growling, which I used to think happened only in cartoons.

Out we went on our usual loop. Before Violet and I could make it far, however, we ran into a neighbor engaged in the same activity and wearing the same who's-the-master-and-who's-the-pet look on her face. Her name is Val.

On a similar walk a few months earlier, Val had inquired about service times and parking at the church where I work. This surprised me, since she had never expressed any interest in the ten years we'd lived in the neighborhood. I gave her the details, and when she did indeed show up the following Sunday, I waved from across the sanctuary. I'd seen her there almost every week since, but we hadn't had any real follow-up.

As soon as she spied me coming her way, Val smiled enthusiastically and said she'd almost emailed me several times but figured our paths—or the paths of our canines—would cross soon enough. She proceeded to gush about how church had become the highlight of her week. She couldn't get enough and seemed almost taken aback by this fact. I asked what made it special.

"Every time I leave that place, I feel so much relief!"

That word again.

I tried to play it cool while my heart leaped inside my chest, and I said a silent prayer of thanksgiving.

After all, this felt like a miracle. We live in a climate rife with statistics about the decline of institutional religion, especially the mainline Protestantism of which my church's denomination is a part. News outlets routinely run reports of younger people leaving the churches in which they were raised in record numbers and checking the "spiritual but not religious" or "none" box on the census form.[3]

While the individual church where I work is thankfully thriving, it cannot be denied that the larger institution of my youth is dying—and dying fast. Those who remain naturally harbor worries about diminishing relevance. People, it appears, are looking elsewhere for meaning and relief.[4]

---

3. See, for example, National Public Radio (NPR), "Religious 'Nones' are now the largest single group in the U.S.," report on *All Things Considered*, January 24, 2024, https://www.npr.org/2024/01/24/1226371734/religious-nones-are-now-the-largest-single-group-in-the-u-s.

4. My abiding impression, however, is that we Westerners aren't any less religious than we always have been; we have just become religious about different things—mainly to our detriment. But that's another book (called *Seculosity*).

7

As dire as it may sound, the decline strikes me as a terrific opportunity for people of faith to reevaluate what they have to offer. What can a person hear, or receive, or participate in at church that they can't find at a good brunch or on a mountain hike? How does what we hear on Sunday differ from what we hear the other six days of the week? What is the church actually doing, and why does it matter?

For years I have watched Christians flail about trying to answer these questions, with varying degrees of success. I've watched conservative Christians pitch family values and personal piety as bulwarks against cultural vacuousness. I've watched progressive Christians focus so much on the church's prophetic witness in matters of social justice that they lose sight of the transcendent. The burdens each camp lays on their adherents are different in substance but not weight. If relief finds its way onto the agenda, it's as a footnote (or something that *those* people need, not us).

I have watched others bang on about community and relationships, still others about self-realization.[5] I've seen Christianity reduced to an intellectual framework and vacuum-sealed away from present-day concerns, a way of worshiping the past or escaping the world. I've also seen the opposite: Christianity subordinated to any number of present-day political ideologies and made into a spiritual accessory to the movement of the moment.

My intention here is not to cast aspersions, or worse, indulge in ungraciousness in the name of grace. Most of these approaches to faith have their merits, especially when we have sufficient energy to give them. Indeed, Christianity has a wide variety of gifts to offer the world. Its ethical vision offers dignity to all people and special consideration of those on the margins. In it we discover a deep well of spiritual resources and tools with which to negotiate the world. Many people find personal purpose in Christianity, whether that be as an outlet for service or a venue for contemplation and mysticism. Still others find guidance via the social order one extrapolates from

5. Enneagram, anyone?

the Bible. All these gifts have much to impart. The problem is that they too easily lose their traction in a person's life when suffering comes, which it inevitably does. When death is staring you in the face, much of the well-meaning noise that fills our pulpits fades into the ether, irrelevant. I wish it weren't so.

But you can find community at a bar. You can find self-realization in therapy. You can find tradition in Nepal. You can find wholesomeness in Utah. You can find political exhortation, well, everywhere. What you find in the Christian faith that you cannot find elsewhere is what my neighbor and plenty other modern people besides have found: the Big Relief of God's saving grace—which is to say, the gospel of Jesus Christ.

Grace is the most important, most urgent, and most radical contribution Christianity has to make to the life of the world—to *your* life and mine! It is what Frederick Buechner calls "a crucial eccentricity of the Christian faith."[6] If you conceive of institutional Christianity as a burning building and you have time to rescue only one item before the edifice collapses, grace is what I would grab every time. There may be more to the way of Jesus than consolation, but there is never less than that. Grace is the emotional engine of the entire works, the too-good-to-be-true-ness at the heart of God.

A Quick Note on Sculptures and Methodology

One last thing before we dash into the burning building: just as *grace* has multiple meanings, so does *relief*. The word refers to something different on a bottle of ibuprofen than it does in a sculptor's studio. A relief is a type of sculpture in which the objects are raised away— but not detached from—a solid surface. The ancient Greeks lined the sides of their temples with reliefs depicting the gods in all sorts of (mis)adventures, a bit like comic strips etched in stone. But you can see relief sculptures in all sorts of places. I think of the incredible

6. Frederick Buechner, *Wishful Thinking: A Seeker's ABC* (HarperCollins, 1993), 38.

art deco relief over the entrance to Rockefeller Center in New York, for example.

This is, presumably, where we derive the figure of speech of one thing being presented "in relief" against another. When we say that a roofline appears in stark relief against the sky, we mean that it sticks out in contrast, delineated, as if situated on a different plane. When we say that a presidential debate put various policies in relief, we mean that the distinctions between competing ideas became clear.

This double meaning applies to grace as well. Grace not only constitutes spiritual relief; it also exists *in relief* against the way life usually works. That is to say, grace runs counter to our instincts about fairness and deserving. It represents an alternative to karmic comeuppance and a break in the cycle of grievance and revenge that dominates human history. Grace jams a stick in the spokes of circular exchange. It is always the exception, which means that no matter how uniquely merciless or contemptuous our present situation may appear, grace has always been in short supply. Its urgency therefore never expires or diminishes.[7]

This is another way of saying that we'll zero in on the Big Relief in part by identifying where it contrasts with the other messages and pressures that surround us. I want to locate where grace departs from how you and I tend to see the world (and how the world tends to see us). To that end, each chapter of this book explores a different dimension of grace.

Maybe one or two will strike you in a fresh way. If they don't, though, I suggest you do what I always do after a bad sermon: find a good place to vent.

---

7. Admittedly, it doesn't always *feel* that way. Part of the impetus behind my writing this book was the perception that we are living in a particularly graceless age. But I suspect most generations have expressed similar sentiments.

1

Grace

The Relief from Deserving

The coach was laying it on a little thick, I thought. This was a tryout for a fifth-grade basketball team, not the NBA. "The truth is, we have a limited number of spots, so I need you to show me why you deserve to be here," he said, channeling Gene Hackman in *Hoosiers*. Geez. This, in a league that made such a big deal of their welcoming ethos, whose website touted that they were interested in the whole person.

I scanned the sidelines and took in the body language of my fellow parents. We were all reliving our own audition experiences. One mother looked particularly uncomfortable. Our kids went to school together, and only the week before she'd complained about the cutthroat competition her older daughter had endured to make the high school dance program. Of course, we'd had that conversation during the reception for the school musical. The consensus among our fellow parents was that the lead role had been given to a teacher's child out of nepotism, not because she had earned it. Not with *that* voice.

All this talk of deserving wasn't limited to my kids' extracurricular activities. A guest at our church's soup kitchen had been told essentially the same thing as those fifth graders when applying for a bed at the local transitional housing facility. He needed to demonstrate why he warranted consideration before his request could move forward. At a wedding a few months previous, my wife and I overheard someone in the row behind us whisper at an awkwardly high volume, "He does not deserve her!"[1] And they were right. The groom was a dope. Maybe his side of the aisle felt the same way about the bride.

I thought of a scene in the television show we had just finished bingeing, *Better Call Saul*. Two brothers, both middle-aged lawyers, sit in a darkened living room. They make small talk about their shared profession, but tension simmers under the surface. Then it explodes. The younger brother, Jimmy, accuses the older brother, Chuck, of blocking an offer for him to work at Chuck's prestigious law firm. "I'm your brother," Jimmy says. "We're supposed to look out for each other. Why were you working against me?"

After a moment of silence, Chuck says, "You're not a real lawyer. University of American Samoa . . . ? An online course? What a joke! I worked my ass off to get where I am. And you take these shortcuts and think suddenly you're my peer. . . . I committed my life to this! You don't slide into it like a cheap pair of slippers and then reap all the rewards."[2]

Chuck shuts down Jimmy's promotion because he feels his brother does not deserve it. Jimmy lacks his older sibling's Ivy League credentials and extensive legal track record. Jimmy has greased all manner of wheels on the way to passing the bar exam. Chuck refuses to let him coast any further up the food chain. Endorsing Jimmy, he believes, would not only cheapen his own life's work but make a mockery of the law itself. And, strictly speaking, he has a point.

The scene marks a definitive falling out between the two men. It's eerily familiar to another spat between siblings over who deserves

---

1. There's also that old chestnut we say about couples we don't like: "They deserve each other!"

2. *Better Call Saul*, season 1, episode 9, "Pimento," directed and written by Thomas Schnauz, aired March 30, 2015, on AMC.

what: the one described in Jesus's parable of the prodigal son (Luke 15:11–32). In both cases, the elder brother is offended by the good fortune shown to his younger sibling. He interprets it as an affront to the hierarchy of deserving on which he has staked his identity. There are no shortcuts to success, right? Everyone must pay their dues. The result is resentment, acrimony, and alienation from both sides.

Of course, you don't have to be embroiled in a Golden Globe–worthy sibling rivalry to see the appeal of such a hierarchy, nor do you have to be interested in keeping others down. A world in which people get what they deserve is a predictable world. It's a manageable one. What it lacks in surprise and flexibility, it makes up for in comprehensibility and safety. Chuck is not crazy.[3]

A hierarchy of deserving is another way of talking about the scales of fairness by which we all abide. If you work hard, you will receive benefits in proportion to your efforts, no more, no less. Reward—financial, reputational, relational—is contingent on exertion. If you put in the hours, you will receive what's owed. If not, you won't. Fair is fair.

Not all hierarchies of deserving rely on effort, though. I cannot help thinking of an episode of another TV show, *Seinfeld*, in which the perennial loser, George Costanza, applies for an apartment in a fancy building, only to find that the co-op board has decided to give it to an older gentleman who survived the *SS Andrea Doria* shipwreck. This man's trauma, presumably, qualifies him for preferential treatment. When George realizes that suffering is their chosen scale of merit, he decides to trot out his own litany of defeats and humiliations. (Jerry: "Your body of work in this field is unparalleled!") He does so in a hilarious montage, leaving the board members speechless and horrified.[4]

It's not just that we believe we deserve something for our hard work; we believe we deserve something for our hard*ships* as well. The

---

3. At least not in respect to Jimmy!

4. *Seinfeld*, season 8, episode 10, "The Andrea Doria," directed by Andy Ackerman, written by Spike Feresten, aired December 19, 1996, on NBC.

more pain we've endured, the more respect and influence we insist should come our way. Even tragedy can be subsumed by competition.

I've heard it said that you can get along with pretty much anyone unless you get in the way of something they feel they deserve or are owed. Emotions run so high because we believe, on some level, that deserving is the chief mode of accumulation available to us, the only reliable way to safeguard our futures. The good things we get in life—respect, wealth, justice, love—will be those things we earn. There is no other route to attainment, short of winning the lottery.[5]

This system offers hope to the qualified, but to their less fortunate cousins, or anyone hobbled by life, it promises a different kind of reciprocity—a pound of flesh, more like. What I'm trying to evoke is the *pressure* of deserving. It is a treadmill we likely take for granted but one that nonetheless runs us ragged, always humming underneath our feet. Can you feel it now?

Fortunately, something exists beyond the horizon of deserving.

A Superabundant Gift

A handful of years ago, theologian John Barclay published an opus titled *Paul and the Gift* in which he traced the contours of grace in the New Testament letters of Saint Paul. What we translate as *grace* was for Paul and his first-century readers the very normal word they used for *gift*. So when Paul talks about the grace of God, he is in large part talking about the gift of God. He is expounding on how and what God gives and to whom. Barclay maintains that the understanding of gift we find in Paul differed from the gift-giving norms

---

5. It could be that I'm describing a particularly modern and Western mode of thinking and that other societies are less meritocratic in their assumptions than mine. Certainly former epochs in history would have taken a more damning view of Jimmy and George: "You were born a peasant—or a noninheriting second sibling—because God (or the gods) have decreed as much. No amount of hard work or ingenuity or suffering is going to change that." I imagine the question of deserving was less active in such settings, at least in an *earthly* sense, reserved mainly for considerations of the afterlife. It's impossible to know for sure.

of the time—or, really, of any time—in several important ways. He calls these distinguishing attributes the "perfections of grace."[6]

For starters, God's grace is fundamentally *incongruous*. Perhaps you remember this word from geometry class. A shape has congruous sides if they match in length. When Barclay says that God's grace is incongruous, he means that the gift does not match the recipient. The gratuity does not match a person's deservingness. There is a marked and even scandalous incongruity between the gift and the person who receives it; the gift's value is not indexed to any perceived worthiness in the recipient. Grace is fundamentally lopsided.

Next, God's grace defies not only our sense of proportion; it defies predictable timing as well. God, in Paul's telling, doesn't give in response to human overtures.[7] He doesn't show grace after we've exhibited proper deference. He gives *first*. This was certainly the case in Paul's own life, when God knocked him off his horse while on his way to Damascus to persecute Christians. Barclay refers to this attribute as the "priority of grace."[8] God takes the first step, lavishing grace on antagonistic men and women before they can prove themselves worthy.

A third defining attribute (or perfection) of God's grace, according to Barclay, has to do with what he terms "superabundance."[9] This refers to the scale of the gift. God does not hold back but exceeds the spending limit by leaps and bounds. There is something overflowing, something mind-bogglingly maximal about the way God gives. In fact, God's gift is excessive to the point that it is personally costly. This isn't a no-skin-off-my-back situation, akin to Scrooge McDuck bulldozing a pile of gold in our direction when there are still mountains of doubloons in the background. No, the giver *feels* it. This means that grace, for it to qualify as divine, involves an element of sacrifice. Barclay identifies several other attributes, but

---

6. John M. G. Barclay, *Paul and the Gift* (Eerdmans, 2015), 70–75.
7. "For while we were still weak, at the right time Christ died for the ungodly" is how Paul puts it in Rom. 5:6.
8. Barclay, *Paul and the Gift*, 71–72.
9. Barclay, *Paul and the Gift*, 70.

the combination of these three—that it is incongruous, prior, and superabundant—provides a helpful entry point to understanding how radical the Bible's understanding of grace really is.

The sportswriter Ryan Hockensmith received a gift like this once. At age seven, he was summoned to the office of Mr. Thompson, the school guidance counselor. They talked for a moment about T-ball, and then Mr. Thompson asked Ryan how things were at home. "Pretty good," he responded, but inside he was panicking. Ryan's dad had recently moved out of their family home. Mr. Thompson didn't push the first grader into talking about it, just smiled and let the boy return to his classroom.

The next day, the loudspeaker summoned Ryan back to Mr. Thompson's office. In a column for ESPN, Ryan recalls what happened: "'Ryan, I have something for you,' Mr. Thompson said, and he slid a 1979 Topps Pedro Guerrero rookie card across his desk to me. Guerrero was my favorite player from my and my dad's favorite team, the Dodgers. . . . 'I'd like to give it to you. Maybe you can hold on to it and remember that if you ever need to talk to someone about anything going on in your life, I'm here.'"

Like magic, the floodgates opened, and young Ryan began to cry for the first and only time during the year when his parents got divorced. Tears of grief, yes, but also tears of relief. He then asked Mr. Thompson the questions he'd been afraid to ask anyone else. Ryan experienced grace in that moment, and it is no accident that it arrived in the form of a gift.[10]

Mr. Thompson's gift fits several if not all of Barclay's descriptors. The Pedro card was superabundant in both its specificity and its size. It conveyed a depth of personal knowledge that was almost unfathomable and, therefore, that much more touching. The card told the young boy that someone saw him, deeply, and cared. But also, Guerrero was an all-star, which meant that his rookie card

---

10. Ryan Hockensmith, "My Priceless, Worthless Baseball Cards," *ESPN*, May 7, 2020, https://www.espn.com/mlb/story/_/id/29143131/150000-worthless-baseball-cards-coronavirus.

would have been worth something. Mr. Thompson would have had to pay a pretty penny for it. Maybe it came from his own collection, in which case he likely felt a pang when he let it go. I would have. Any Pedro card would have been well-received, but the rookie one? You can almost hear the kid's head explode.

The gift also came as a complete surprise. Never in a million years would Ryan have seen it coming. Mr. Thompson gave it before—or prior to—any expression of need or desire on Ryan's part. When we talk about grace catching us off guard and by surprise, we are often referring to its priority.

Furthermore, if Ryan expected anything as he ambled to the office, it wasn't the card of his dreams. Every kid knows that calls to the front office are usually the precursor to punishment. Maybe Ryan thought he was in trouble for not being up front with Mr. Thompson in their first meeting. But even if that trepidation didn't register in a seven-year-old's brain, Ryan's internal reality was likely one of confusion and shame—divorce was more stigmatized in the 1980s, when this took place. Yet instead of a pep talk or lecture, he received Pedro Guerrero. Incongruous in the extreme!

Crucially, the gesture was also *noncontingent*, which is a further adjective we might add to our emerging lexicon of grace. The card was not given with the expectation of a certain reaction from Ryan, or to butter him up to take part in some program. It wasn't a hidden bribe or means of manipulation. It was a gift, pure and simple, not a token of appreciation but a talisman of grace. No doubt that's why Ryan found himself writing about it more than thirty years later.

Such a gift stands in stark relief to the season we typically associate with gift-giving. Take, for instance, what may be the most subversive song ever written: "Santa Claus Is Comin' to Town." It's not subversive for the reasons that religious people typically lament the detour from Bethlehem to the North Pole—that is, commercialization and secularization. The song is subversive because of how it sabotages the beating heart of Christmas, which has to do with giving.

"Santa Claus Is Comin' to Town" paints a picture of pure congruity, pure contingency: "He's making a list / He's checking it twice / He's gonna find out / Who's naughty and nice."[11] Nice children get appropriately nice toys; naughty ones get lumps of coal. Santa Claus may have a sack full of shiny packages, but they are not gifts, at least not in the New Testament sense. He's handing out rewards for good behavior. Gifts premised on deserving aren't gifts at all; they are more like paychecks, gestures based in reciprocity rather than generosity. I doubt the songwriters were trying to be subversive, though. They were simply articulating the logic of quid pro quo that's instinctual to every human heart.

When the Script Flips

The podcast *Invisibilia* once put out an episode that explored the miracle of incongruity in less theological but no less gracious terms. At the beginning of the episode titled "Flip the Script," a man named Michael Rabdou recounts a warm summer night in the not-so-distant past when he and a group of friends were enjoying dinner and drinks in a backyard in Washington, DC. Around 10:00 p.m., they were interrupted by an intruder. This man pointed a gun at Rabdou's friend and demanded money. No one had any cash on them, so they fervently began trying to dissuade the guy, appealing to his conscience. He responded to their pleas with hostility. It looked like things were about to escalate in a terrible direction.

Just then, a woman named Christina piped up. She told the interloper that they were in the midst of a celebration and asked if he would like a glass of wine. Rabdou reports that the man's countenance immediately shifted. Indeed, the whole tenor of the encounter softened. The group watched as the man tasted the wine and slowly put the gun away. Then he said something shocking: "I think I've come to the wrong place. . . . Can I get a hug?"

11. "Santa Claus Is Comin' to Town," by John Frederick Coots and Haven Gillespie, Leo Feist Inc., 1934.

Before they had time to think about it, the dinner guests formed a circle and hugged the person who had been threatening them mere seconds ago. He muttered an apology and left the way he came. Rabdou says, "It was like a miracle." No "like" about it—grace is miraculous.

Make no mistake: the offer of wine was an act of grace. It was thoroughly incongruous to the man's aggressive behavior. Christina offered it to him while his gun was still raised—that is, before he indicated any willingness to engage. Nor was the drink part of some bartering scheme. Christina did not say, "You can have some wine if you drop the gun." No doubt a lowered firearm was the hope, but she somehow had the presence of mind not to phrase it that way. Turning the overture into a transaction would have undercut the abundance of her generosity.

To shed light on this remarkable reversal, host Alix Spiegel interviews a psychologist, Christopher Hopwood, who introduces her to the concept of noncomplementary behavior. According to Hopwood, human beings naturally mirror one another's behavior. If someone gives us the benefit of the doubt in a discussion, we tend to give it back to them. "Warmth begets warmth," he says. On the flip side, if someone acts aggressively toward us on the highway, we usually respond in kind, possibly with a rude hand gesture, possibly by refusing to let them merge when traffic slows. Breaking the pattern is both difficult and uncommon.

Fortunately, as the story testifies, every so often people manage to behave in noncomplementary ways. When this happens, the ground of predictability shakes, and new fissures of possibility open. Our instinctive mirroring takes a new course. Hopwood ascribes this rare ability to moral exemplars like Mahatma Gandhi and Martin Luther King Jr., who "were able to maintain a sort of warmth and integrity in the face of people who were being cruel to them."[12] If

12. Alix Spiegel, with Lulu Miller and Hanna Rosin, "Flip the Script," *Invisibilia* podcast, NPR, July 15, 2016, https://www.npr.org/programs/invisibilia/485603559/flip-the-script.

that sounds like another historical figure who habitually turned the other cheek, we'll get there.

You Are Not Michael Jordan

The voices we hear six days a week, from outside and in, tell us that the happy things we get will be the happy things we merit. This is good news to those blessed with energy, education, and talent—the Michael Jordans and Steph Currys of the world who thrive under pressure. The logic of deserving can take such individuals far, sometimes as far as the last dance. Sadly, it has at least four whopping limitations.

First, if deserving is the primary rubric through which we understand life, then not only are we to be praised when good fortune arrives but we are also to be blamed when bad fortune does. It will be very hard not to see suffering, in some way, as our fault. Punishment is the shadow side of reward. You can't really embrace the gratification of one without the tyranny of the other.

Second, when the day comes that our ability and resolve falter—when we make the easy choice instead of the right one—our hopes for the future will not be far behind in faltering with them. If goodness and security are reserved for the deserving, we better not let our performance slip. Yet, everyone's abilities falter eventually; such is the nature of mortality. When peace and hope are linked to merit, before long they will evaporate entirely.

Third, the measures we use to weigh deserving are invariably skewed. This could have to do with changing social norms, such as the way we once valued the liberal arts but now almost exclusively laud practical, marketable know-how in college grads. It could be related to the limits of our vision. Our neighbor may lose our respect when he gets fired from his job, but we're ignorant of the fact that he missed those deadlines because he was caring for a dying relative. Conversely, we may envy our other neighbor because of her promotion, but we're ignorant of the colleagues she threw under the bus to get it. We never have enough data to make unassailable judgments of who deserves what.

Fourth, those who operate strictly according to a scale of deserving are insufferable and often cruel, to both others and themselves. Can you imagine a parent not giving a birthday present to their problem child? In the 2022 documentary *Stutz*, the actor Jonah Hill outlines a past injustice to his therapist, the titular Stutz. Jonah can't stop ruminating on one particular slight that has gone unpunished. Stutz declares, "Your quest for fairness is keeping your life on hold."[13] Jonah's insistence on quid pro quo has trapped him in resentment. To move on and heal, he must renounce his fixation on deserving.

Christianity does not echo the injunction to get out there and take what's ours (and not let anyone get in our way). Instead, it has the audacity to claim the opposite: any good thing that you're going to get in life is going to be something you *receive*. Existence itself is something given to us rather than earned by us. Furthermore, the incarnate Son of God represents *pure* gift, a light shining on those who dwell in darkness, the revelation of God's love in all its vulnerability and impossibility. Like all great gifts, he arrives in that stable unbidden and of God's own initiative—a sweet and glorious surprise to a world that lay "in sin and error pining."[14] Those familiar with the rest of the Bible know that Jesus was anything but a reward for human obedience and faithfulness.

In his life and ministry, Jesus Christ bore out this divine gift incongruity. He became a walking embodiment of it. Those who welcomed him most enthusiastically were the ones whose lives had stripped them of any illusions about what they deserved. He sought them out too. "It is not the healthy who need a doctor, but the sick. I have not come to call the righteous, but sinners," Jesus said by way of a mission

13. *Stutz*, directed by Jonah Hill (Strong Baby Productions, 2022), Netflix, https://www.netflix.com/title/81387962.

14. This phrase comes from the Christmas carol "O Holy Night," originally written by Placide Cappeau and Adolphe Adam in 1847 and translated into English by John Sullivan Dwight in 1855. My favorite version is the one recorded by the band Duvall for their 2004 album, *O Holy Night*.

statement (Mark 2:17 NIV). It seems he was interested in people whose *only* way of receiving him was as a gift. This is what we see in his treatment of lepers and tax collectors and prostitutes and reprobates; Jesus does not relate to them on the basis of what they bring to the table but on the basis of who he is. God's grace, as revealed in Jesus Christ, is not tied to any human criterion of worth. If anything, God inverts our precious hierarchy of deserving and behaves in the most noncomplementary fashion imaginable, giving superabundant attention, approval, and love—his very self—to the wrong sort of people.[15] Like Christina at that fateful backyard soirée, God surprises his enemies with blessing before they even know what hit them.

God Is Not Betty Crocker

The work of a Christian, then, to the extent it can be called work, is to empty one's hands so they are open to receive grace. This may sound straightforward, but we often resist receptivity. It can be a very uncomfortable position for a species habituated to reward. We much prefer congruity, contingency, and complementarity. Betty Crocker learned this lesson the hard way.

In 1947, General Mills launched a new line of Betty Crocker instant cake mixes that tasted almost as good as the stuff made from scratch. Though the cake mixes were incredibly popular at first, sales soon slowed, and the corporation couldn't understand why. They were providing a good product at a fair price and making homemakers' lives easier in the process. The trickling-off defied common sense.

Legend has it that General Mills enlisted a Freudian psychologist to help them figure it out. The analyst concluded that the decline

---

15. See also Rom. 4:2–5, in which Paul parses God's radically generous treatment of Abraham. Despite the patriarch's ungodliness, Abraham is the recipient of God's gift through faith: "For if Abraham was justified by works, he has something to boast about, but not before God. For what does the scripture say? 'Abraham believed God, and it was reckoned to him as righteousness.' Now to one who works, wages are not reckoned as a gift but as something due. But to one who does not work but trusts him who justifies the ungodly, such faith is reckoned as righteousness."

in sales was a result of guilt. If all that consumers were doing was adding water, they felt less ownership of the cake, less pride. The homemakers in question didn't feel like they could tell their families it was homemade. So they stopped buying the mix.

In a flash of brilliance, General Mills pivoted their strategy, relaunching the product with a new slogan, "Add an Egg." Baking was still easy, but the cook had a little more to do. The mix now required them to mix in an egg of their own. Profits skyrocketed.[16]

The initial attempt at a cake mix forced would-be bakers into a state of receptivity, denying them the sense that their efforts were needed—that their contribution mattered. The egg, while technically unnecessary, was just enough to restore that sense. The egg dampened the blow of incongruity. It allowed homemakers to take some credit. They now felt like they *deserved* their family's appreciation. One assumes that those who couldn't afford eggs were less enthusiastic about the update.

I am reminded of the tongue-in-cheek prayer that author and theologian Robert Capon composed to illustrate the exasperation and even terror we feel when confronted with the egglessness, so to speak, of God's grace: "Restore to us, Preacher, the comfort of merit and demerit. Prove for us that there is at least something we can do, that we are still, at whatever dim recess of our nature, the masters of our relationships. Tell us, Prophet, that in spite of all our nights of losing, there will yet be one redeeming card of our very own to fill the inside straight we have so long and so earnestly tried to draw to. But do not preach us grace. . . . Give us something, anything; but spare us the indignity of this indiscriminate acceptance."[17] You could sub out Capon's phrase "indiscriminate acceptance" for "incongruous gift," and the meaning would hold. Grace is an affront to the deserving, but to the empty-handed, it is the Big Relief.

16. Amanda Montell, *The Age of Magical Overthinking* (Simon & Schuster, 2024), 208–9.

17. Robert Farrar Capon, *Between Noon and Three* (Eerdmans, 1997), 7–8.

Of course, we can resist receptivity all we want, but life has a way of vacating our hands. Circumstances will jostle and disorient us, such that our precious eggs fall to the ground and break. Yet if God gives the way the Bible says he does, that may not be such a bad position to be in. God betrays our allegiance to deserving. Just ask my childhood hero, Darryl Strawberry.

The Saint of Second Chances

I grew up in the 1980s in a suburb of New York City situated, baseball-wise, squarely in Mets territory. If I had found myself in the same position as Ryan Hockensmith, the gift that would have unlocked my heart (and tears) would've been Darryl Strawberry's 1983 Topps Traded rookie card. Strawberry was not just a superstar but a superhero, especially after the Mets won the World Series in 1986.

Sadly, as is often the case, the combination of celebrity, youth, and bottomless cash proved to be a curse as much as a blessing to Strawberry. The Mets had gained their reputation as the bad boys of baseball for good reason. For Strawberry, this involved abusing narcotics. The addiction soon fueled all sorts of antisocial behavior. By 1994, it had ravaged his life to the extent that he lost a multimillion-dollar contract with the San Francisco Giants. He also lost his endorsement deals, the adoration of the public, his marriage, and custody of his children. Suddenly, no one would hire one of the biggest stars on the planet. After the Giants let him go, he was turned down by 206 teams—incidentally, the number of bones in the human body.

Enter minor league impresario Mike Veeck, someone familiar with engineering one's own demise. Veeck had started out his career working in the Chicago White Sox front office but had been fired after orchestrating the infamous Disco Demolition Night fiasco at Comiskey Park in 1979.[18] After that catastrophe, Veeck fell into a

18. Disco Demolition Night was a promotion held by the White Sox for their doubleheader on July 12, 1979, in which admission was offered for only ninety-eight cents to anyone who brought a disco record with them. The records were collected at the gate and put into

lengthy season of addiction. It had taken years, but somehow he re-
gained a semblance of stature by helming the St. Paul Saints, a minor
league team known for their outlandish promotions and circus-like
atmosphere.

When no one would give Strawberry a "fourth second chance,"
Veeck, at the urging of his wife, Libby, offered the downtrodden star
a contract to play for the Saints in 1996. Considering how many
times Veeck himself had been on the receiving end of undeserved
opportunity, he couldn't *not* do so. He put his own reputation on
the line to sign Strawberry and thereby gift the struggling slugger
a fresh start.

But St. Paul is a long way from San Francisco. Professionally
speaking, it was the end of the line, a club populated by players (and
commentators and owners and mascots) whom no one else would
take. They may as well have been called the St. Paul Empty-Handed.
Yet it was there that Strawberry made friends with Dave Stevens,
an outfielder who had been born without legs. Stevens's gratitude
and good cheer, despite a disability that many would view as a non-
starter in the national pastime, pierced the fallen superstar's sullen
demeanor. Stevens's ebullient perspective jolted Strawberry out of
his self-pity and reminded him how fun it is to play baseball. Their
friendship became the catalyst for something new in the slugger's
life. In a documentary about the team released in 2023, *The Saint
of Second Chances*, Strawberry tells the camera, "I realized I'm just
not that darn important."

When the wider world was telling Darryl Strawberry that he
deserved nothing but scorn (and possibly jail time), the repeat of-
fender from the Big Apple experienced the Big Relief in St. Paul.
Incongruously, and superabundantly, he received gratitude, joy, and
a future where none had been before. Soon Strawberry was back in

---

crates to be detonated by Chicago disc jockey Steve Dahl in between games. Far more people
showed up than could fit into the stadium or the security could handle. After the explosion
a riot ensued, and the park was badly damaged. The event has since come to be seen as an
ugly display of anti-Black and anti-gay sentiment, since those were the subcultures most
closely associated with the genre.

the majors, winning two more World Series before retiring in 2000 and eventually becoming a pastor. His portion of the documentary ends with him saying, "I didn't want to be a superstar anymore. I just wanted to be."[19]

Those sure sound like the words of a saint to me.

19. *The Saint of Second Chances*, directed by Jeff Malmberg and Morgan Neville (Tremolo Productions, 2023), Netflix, https://www.netflix.com/title/81476121.

2

Forgiveness

The Relief from Regret

Fifty years is a long time to hold on to a library book, even one as good as James Hilton's *Goodbye, Mr. Chips*. So imagine the surprise of some librarians in Queens when, in late 2021, they opened a package containing a copy of Hilton's novella that had been checked out of the branch back in 1970. The address under which it had been originally borrowed had become a shopping plaza. Um, thanks?

The timing wasn't random. *Mr. Chips* was one of nearly ninety thousand titles returned to the New York Public Library (NYPL) system during the six-month period following the NYPL's decision to discontinue penalties for overdue books and to forgive all existing fines. The NYPL had been contemplating the move for some time, watching as other municipalities took the leap.[1] Of course, there were financial obstacles to overcome. In 2019, the system had collected about $3 million in late fees, and that revenue would have to be made

---

1. In the first three weeks after Chicago introduced the same policy, they saw a 240 percent increase in return of materials as well as four hundred more card renewals compared with the same period during the previous year. Emma Bowman, "'We Wanted Our Patrons Back'—Public Libraries Scrap Late Fines to Alleviate Inequity," NPR, November 30, 2019, https://www.npr.org/2019/11/30/781374759/we-wanted-our-patrons-back-public-libraries -scrap-late-fines-to-alleviate-inequi.

up for in some other way. The library president was confident they could adjust their budget, stating, "We are not in the fine-collection business. We're in the encouraging-to-read-and-learn business."[2]

The gamble worked. After the announcement, not only did long-lost books pour back in, long-lost patrons did too. The district saw a 9–15 percent increase in returning visitors, many of whom had had their privileges revoked because of the standing balances on their accounts. With records expunged, the forgiven patrons were free to enjoy the library again.

Forgiven is the right word. One way to understand forgiveness is as the foregoing of restitution. The NYPL waived their right to collect what they were rightfully owed. In doing so, they not only erased the debt but also reinstated the memberships of suspended patrons. Forgiveness ushered in a restored relationship, as it often does.

A few patrons voiced objections: What would keep people from absconding with library materials going forward? For the most part, though, the public greeted the change with open arms. Libraries are supposed to be free, after all.

The same cannot be said for a high-profile instance of debt forgiveness that occurred about two years earlier. Midway through his 2019 commencement address to the graduates of Morehouse College, billionaire investor Robert F. Smith announced that he would personally pay off the student loan balance of the entire graduating class. By aiding nearly four hundred young men at the historically Black all-men's college to the tune of nearly $40 million, his donation was the biggest single gift in the school's 152-year history.

A third party wiping the slate clean by absolving an incurred debt—by surprise, without coercion, and at a cost to themselves—is what we call an act of grace. The graduates themselves were understandably thrilled and deeply relieved. They had been liberated from the crushing weight of those loans, which could have followed them

2. Gina Cherelus, "The Library Ends Late Fees, and the Treasures Roll In," *New York Times*, April 1, 2022, https://www.nytimes.com/2022/03/31/nyregion/nyc-library-fines-books-returned.html.

around for decades and confined all sorts of future decisions. These young men were now free to follow the path in front of them—maybe take a more interesting but lower-paying job—independent of concerns about compounding interest. They might take a professional risk they otherwise wouldn't have with a loan balance in the back of their minds. At the least, they'd be able to buy a house sooner.

Those on the outside were less enthusiastic. Criticism of Smith came fast and furious. Some lambasted his gesture as shortsighted and not sufficiently systemic. Most took issue with what they perceived as unfairness. Michelle Singletary at the *Washington Post* relayed this response: "Of course, I'm happy for the students and am very appreciative of a rich person who contributes from his success to others. However, my immediate thought was: 'What about the classmates who struggled and sacrificed to pay the cost of their education without going into debt?' There must be many feeling left out, unlucky, or even resentful."[3] These objections are nothing if not sensible.

It wasn't just that Smith's forgiveness excluded past and future graduating classes at the university. The deeper complaint had to do with the perception that he had validated irresponsibility. To some onlookers, student loan debt is symbolic of poor decisions, an excessively loose attitude toward finances and the future. The students who need loans, the thinking goes, must come from families who have squandered resources on immediate gratification rather than maintaining the more difficult discipline of saving. As such, those students do not deserve Smith's generosity, right? An anonymous reader wrote that the students "racked up debt with no idea of how they could minimize it or how they would pay it off and are being rewarded for irresponsible financial behavior."[4]

3. Michelle Singletary, "Robert Smith Pledged to Pay Off Morehouse Graduates' Student Loans. Is This Fair to Families Who Saved?," *Washington Post*, May 23, 2019, https://www.washingtonpost.com/business/2019/05/23/robert-smith-pledged-pay-off-morehouse-graduates-student-loans-is-this-fair-families-who-saved/.
4. Singletary, "Morehouse Graduates' Student Loans."

What these objections miss is that forgiveness is, by definition, undeserved. If Smith had singled out the most hardworking and self-sacrificing graduates (and their families), the donation would have been more of a prize than an act of grace.

The offensiveness is worth noting. To those in need, forgiveness comes as a relief. To others, it comes as an affront.

The Past Is Never Past?

The relief of forgiveness thankfully extends beyond the financial realm. Generally speaking, forgiveness represents a merciful response to the pressure exerted by an imperfect past. Since no one's past is immaculate, everyone deals with this pressure to some extent or another, consciously or not. Debt may be the presenting circumstance here, but it could just as well be accident, disappointment, or wrongdoing that's weighing us down. Financial debt is a useful case in point since so many of us are familiar with it. Credit card balances, medical bills, car payments, mortgages—these things are everywhere. Likely there is some outstanding balance in your life that, were it to be forgiven, would award you an easier night's sleep. But there are other kinds of debts. When someone is convicted of a crime, for example, we speak of the debt they owe to society.

The most dramatic instances of forgiveness, in fact, have to do with crime and atrocity. I think of Cancilde, the Rwandan widow whose husband and five of her seven children were killed during the genocide some thirty years ago. The killer was one of their neighbors, a young man named Emmanuel, and about a year after the murders he was arrested and sent to prison. Following his release in 2003, Emmanuel sought out Cancilde and begged her to have mercy on him. Inspired by the Bible study she faithfully attended with other widows, Cancilde defied the wisdom of her neighbors and forgave Emmanuel to his face.[5]

5. Denise Uwimana, *From Red Earth* (Plough, 2019), 197–98.

That's not where the story ends, though. In 2015, fellow survivor Denise Uwimana visited their region as part of her research for a book, *From Red Earth*, about the aftermath of the genocide. She spoke with Emmanuel and Cancilde and discovered that the forgiveness ran much deeper than a onetime pronouncement. Uwimana recounts their exchange:

> "Cancilde has become like a mother to me," [Emmanuel] said quietly. "When I need advice, I go to her. Before I got married, I talked over the details with her. She is the local official who authorized my marriage."
>
> Cancilde broke in, "Emmanuel is the one I ask for help when my house needs repair. He comes any time I ask, to replace a window or mend the roof. If my cow has problems, I call him. And he knows he's always welcome to share a meal at my home. . . . He is my son!"[6]

Reading about their relationship brings tears to my eyes. I need to hear such stories, not only because they put my own grievances into perspective but because they testify that there is nowhere the Big Relief cannot reach, no damage so deep or ghastly it cannot be healed. Such stories inspire hope. They suggest that no matter who we are or what we've done—or what's been done to us—we need not be defined by the worst day of our lives. Forgiveness may be a miracle, but that doesn't mean it's unavailable.

And yet I wonder if there is a danger in dwelling on dramatic instances of forgiveness. If nothing near that level of severity has transpired in our lives, we can all too easily "compare out." "I haven't ever gotten into a fight, let alone killed someone," we might think. "So what does forgiveness have to do with me?" Maybe our upbringing was fairly tranquil and our adulthood uneventful. We haven't been the targets of malice, nor can we recall committing any crimes,

6. Denise Uwimana, "How Far Does Forgiveness Reach? Emmanuel and Cancilde, Neighbors on Opposite Sides of the Rwandan Genocide, Tell Their Story," *Plough*, April 11, 2024, https://www.plough.com/en/topics/life/forgiveness/how-far-does-forgiveness -reach.

relational or otherwise. We haven't experienced any major bumps in the road where forgiveness might be called for. That level of smooth sailing may be rare, but hey, all power to you.

Alas, you may be able to escape catastrophe, but no one escapes the unchangeability of the past. No one dodges regret completely. We all have some moment we would redo if given the chance, some past decision or utterance we would take back if we could. It could be a specific memory that makes us cringe in embarrassment. But it could equally be the way we treated our younger sibling when we were growing up, whether that be with overt bullying or casual indifference.[7] Maybe we failed to spend time with an aging relative before they passed. Maybe we wish we'd saved more money or taken better care of our body. We may not be talking about sin per se, but we are nonetheless in the territory of forgiveness. The burden of the past weighs on us all—no matter how mundane our failures or minor our missteps—and cries out for reconciliation. It certainly does for me.

Just after I started to take my Christian faith seriously as a young adult, I attended a get-together with my high school friends. We hadn't seen one another for a year or two at that point and were excited to have a few days together to gallivant around New York City. One of my closest friends from those days is Phil. Phil's greatest passion in life was playing heavy metal music (technically, "thrash metal"). He was the singer in a group that had toured around the country and put out a couple of albums. As his friends, we cheered him on, even if the music itself was a little scary.

During the reunion, after one beer too many and for some reason I still don't understand—insecurity most likely—I decided I would grill my buddy about the musical genre to which he was devoting

---

7. I was terrible to my younger brother during our adolescence. I'd belittle him when I felt bad about myself, sometimes using my fists to drive the point home. I regret it every day. Instead of a toast at the rehearsal dinner for his wedding, I issued a public apology for the harm I caused. He'd already forgiven me many times over, but it felt good to say it in front of others. My only consolation up to that point was that he'd written his college essay about how I bullied him—and it had gotten him into Harvard. Woof.

his life. Wasn't metal emotionally monochrome? Luxuriating in that much aggression can't be healthy, right? Looking back, I realize I was working out my own relationship, as a new Christian, to the hard rock I had grown up loving.[8] But I engaged Phil not out of curiosity so much as out of judgment. In short, I was a total jerk and lost a friend that night. It didn't help that I also transgressed my own ideals as an all-opportunity music obsessive.

Five years later, when I moved to the city after getting married, the regret lingered. It had actually metastasized a little. Phil was living there, so finally, at the urging of my wife, I sent him a message and asked if we could get lunch. Over dumplings, I told him I was wrong about what I had said back then, confessing that I'd even sung karaoke to Dio's "Holy Diver" at my bachelor party. I asked if he could forgive me. Phil confirmed that my words had hurt him— coming from out of the blue as they did—and that he had missed our friendship. He forgave me. It may seem like a small thing, but it was a big deal to me.[9] I felt lighter leaving that lunch, not least because I could finally listen to my beloved Alice in Chains without feeling like a total hypocrite.

Again, our regrets can be big or small—something we've done or left undone—but it's impossible to go through life without incurring a few. This means that we all come into contact with forgiveness sooner or later. No wonder writer Elizabeth Bruenig defines *forgiveness* as "a process that unites wronged and wrongdoer in a plan of peace," adding that "since we've all been on both sides of that equation hoping for the same thing, it seems a most useful virtue."[10]

---

8. That is, could I love God and Axl Rose at the same time? Should I? (Answer: *Could* and *should* are moot. I did and do.) See my book, *A Mess of Help: From the Crucified Soul of Rock n' Roll* (Mockingbird, 2014).

9. I sometimes wonder if smaller instances of forgiveness are equally miraculous: the wife who forgives her husband his snoring, her sister-in-law her bad breath, her neighbors their weird recycling habits.

10. Elizabeth Bruenig, "The Limits of Forgiveness," *Point*, April 5, 2023, https://thepoint mag.com/examined-life/the-limits-of-forgiveness/.

Zeros and Ones Never Forget

The topic of regret has taken on a different color since the advent of the internet—for both better and worse. It is harder to polish the past when there's a record of blemishes for anyone with a keyboard to access. Injustices cannot be ignored or glossed over with the same ease. The narratives we weave to justify our missteps, consciously and unconsciously, can be checked against what actually happened. This innovation is of pressing aid to those who have felt bamboozled by people in power. The result can be an increase in justice, such as the right (guilty) person going before the Rwandan tribunal to face their crimes rather than an innocent bystander. Another potential result would be an increase in compassion, as in, "I wasn't imagining how terribly that person treated me! My wounds aren't as fictitious or self-imposed as I was led to believe." The ever-present past can be helpful to those harboring concrete regrets as well. The unvarnished truth is never an enemy so long as it serves as a fresh opportunity for humility, contrition and, God willing, forgiveness. As Bruenig reminds us, we've all been—or will be—on both sides of the equation.

Of course, there is an indisputable dark side to this elephant-like digital memory. I graduated from college in 2001. Napster had been around for a while, but Twitter was several years away. OkCupid and Match.com wouldn't rear their heads until after most of my cohort had paired off, and even then, it took nearly a decade before online dating experienced much acceptance in the mainstream. I once heard a friend say that dating during the early 2000s was like getting the last chopper out of Vietnam. We didn't know it at the time, but Tinder and other dating apps were about to carpet-bomb the romantic landscape, leaving it a dehumanized husk of its former self.

But that's not the only chopper we hitched before the terrain shifted. On the sidelines of our kids' soccer games, my peers and I bond over how grateful we are that no one had smartphones when we were growing up. Our gratitude has nothing to do with the lack of distraction we (apparently) experienced. No, we are thankful we were allowed to do the stupid things that teenagers do without worrying about being captured on camera. In the '90s, rumors could and would spread as they always have, but we did not have to deal with the threat of our most juvenile exploits going viral and following us into perpetuity. We took for granted the freedom to be nineteen-year-old doofuses.

Young people today contend with the permanence of their mistakes in new and frightening ways. Indeed, lapses in judgment—an insensitive tweet, a regrettable photo—can stick around long after the collective attention shifts, ready to be answered for at job interviews and first dates for the next twenty years. What feels empowering when it comes to holding bullies (and politicians and celebrities and even clergy) to account for their bad behavior takes on a harsher light when applied to the tenth grader who put something reckless online after drinking beer for the first time. The archiving of our lives can serve, in other words, as an obstacle to mercy and healing just as readily as it can to dishonesty and self-justification.[11] Whatever the case, the past exerts added pressure on everyone.

It could be that the landscape has evolved further—meaning, the danger of digital permanence isn't so much the dredging up of past missteps but the present withdrawal. During COVID-19, when classes at the university in our town went virtual, an undergraduate I know told me that he'd stopped volunteering to read any of his responses to the assigned texts in his psychology seminar for fear that those germinal thoughts—not yet fully formed and therefore ideal for discussion—would be screenshotted and used to shame him. Of course, this chilling effect has extended into nonclassroom spheres as well. No one wants an ill-considered moment to end up on TikTok; better to guard every syllable and never risk vulnerability.

Given the ubiquity of such tools, we are tempted to believe we live in a uniquely unforgiving moment. We do not. The human race has

11. I don't mean to suggest that doofus-like behavior can't turn scarring and serious in the blink of an eye, or that regret and repentance aren't essential to growing up. They undoubtedly are. But I'm also wary of the human inclination to dress up vengeance in the language of justice. As someone who lived through a pre-Zuckerberg adolescence, I can't pretend I don't wish my children had the same privilege. We certainly didn't realize that forgettability *was* a privilege.

never suffered from an overabundance of mercy in our relationships. Our devices have simply made it easier to keep our scorecards of personal and social righteousness close at hand. Put another way, Silicon Valley did not invent the human impulse to judge and categorize and punish; it just made the most efficient and effective machines to harness those impulses.

Australian musician and indie hero Nick Cave sums up what we lose when unforgiveness becomes too convenient: "Mercy ultimately acknowledges that we are all imperfect and in doing so allows us the oxygen to breathe—to feel protected within a society, through our mutual fallibility. Without mercy a society loses its soul, and devours itself. . . . Without mercy society grows inflexible, fearful, vindictive and humorless."[12] Perhaps this is part of what Thomas Merton meant when he wrote, long before the web was a gleam in Al Gore's eye, "In hell there is everything but mercy."[13]

This need not be cause for dismay. For purveyors of the Big Relief, the mercilessness of the digital sphere represents an opportunity. If the past stands ready to condemn us at the click of a button, the prospect of thoroughgoing forgiveness holds that much more appeal. Forgiveness involves, after all, the willingness not to hold a person's past against them.

A therapist once told me that the best marriages she knew were the ones in which people had figured out a way to let go of the past. The most lasting, loving relationships, in other words, are grounded in forgiveness. And the opposite of forgiveness isn't debt or credit but resentment, which we refer to today colloquially as grudge holding.[14] Relationships where the past is overactive, where old injuries are trotted out at a moment's notice, are relationships that end.

Christians believe that forgiveness lies at the heart of God and, therefore, the heart of love.

---

12. Nick Cave, "What Is Mercy for You?," *Red Hand Files*, August 2020, https://www.theredhandfiles.com/what-is-mercy-for-you/.

13. Thomas Merton, *New Seeds of Contemplation* (Shambhala Publications, 1961), 93.

14. Cue the *Onion*'s "Heartfelt Apology Robs Man of Cherished Grudge," June 10, 2010, https://www.theonion.com/heartfelt-apology-robs-man-of-cherished-grudge-1819571566.

What Forgiveness Isn't

Like *grace*, the word *forgiveness* radiates positivity and meaning. It towers so high that it can be confusing to discern its contours. Something that's often mistaken for forgiveness, for instance, is mitigation. Mitigation involves the attempt to put wrongdoing in context, usually by invoking the wrongdoer's circumstances: "You hurt me, but I understand you did it because you had been hurt in such-and-such a way yourself." Mitigation locates sympathy with victimizers by highlighting the ways in which they themselves have been victimized, which in turn qualifies their responsibility for what happened. You realize they are not truly culpable for hurting you— society is the problem, or the person's family, or the church in which they were raised. In this way, mitigation shrinks the infraction, such that understanding and empathy are needed rather than absolution. Such considerations often bring us closer to a posture of forgiveness. Yet forgiveness goes further than mitigation. It persists in the absence of mitigating factors, covering our transgressions in mercy, regardless of the circumstances and motivations that informed those transgressions.

People sometimes worry that advocating for forgiveness in a situation is tantamount to diminishing the harm that's been done, or implying the wrongdoing didn't matter. But forgiveness doesn't diminish wrongdoing—if anything, it amplifies it. It says that understanding and empathy *aren't* enough to heal what's been done.

Another way we twist forgiveness and take away the relief it brings has to do with apology. We make repentance a precondition for pardon. We insist that people express sufficient remorse before we reconcile. In religious terms, human sorrow becomes the key that unlocks divine pardon. Alas, the stipulation tends to flatten forgiveness into something overly transactional. And even if it didn't, what constitutes sufficient remorse? Moreover, how do you know if someone's sorrow is sincere? Is forgiveness limited to only those things about which we feel adequately apologetic? The challenges are myriad.

If the forgiveness we've been tracing sounds daunting, it should. The type of forgiveness at the heart of the Big Relief isn't just rare or challenging; humanly speaking, it is impossible. This is why Christians believe that true forgiveness is a miracle. When it happens—and it does!—it is the work of God.

As with most other avenues of grace, we like forgiveness—in theory; namely, we like it when we're the ones being forgiven. We like it less when it's reaching toward those who have done us personal wrong. When it comes to our enemies, in fact, we tend to hate forgiveness. We fear that it lets bad actors off the hook and thereby encourages continued oppression, discord, and taking advantage. We worry that forgiveness allows cycles of injustice and abuse to continue.[15] And to be sure, the way some Christian communities have taught forgiveness—as a command to remain with an abusive spouse, say—transforms something intended to offer freedom and joy into another moral duty that has real victims. There is something inherently scandalous about forgiveness, but the scandal is not that the hurting party continues being hurt. The scandal is that the guilty party is given a clemency they do not deserve.

This was certainly true in Jesus's time. One of the most beautiful episodes of forgiveness in the Gospels comes in Luke 7:36–50. Jesus has been invited to dinner at the house of an esteemed religious leader named Simon. After they sit down to eat, a woman interrupts their meal. Luke describes her as someone who "lived a sinful life" (NIV), implying she is not the sort of person who would normally be welcome at the home of a Pharisee. If she speaks any words after barging in, Luke doesn't record them. Instead, he records what she does. The woman approaches Jesus and starts weeping so heavily that her tears wet his feet. She proceeds to wipe his feet clean with her hair, kissing and anointing them with expensive perfume. It is about as emotional a display of reverence as one could imagine, no doubt an awkward interlude in what was supposed to be a proper dinner. Jesus does not rebuke her.

15. As those librarians in Queens discovered, it is actually the *absence* of forgiveness that accomplishes dehumanization. Witness every comment thread on every YouTube video.

Simon, the host, responds with incredulity, muttering to himself about how insulted Jesus should be, given this woman's reputation. Jesus picks up on the reproach and lectures the supposedly holy men on the holiness of the woman's public outpouring. They haven't shown him an ounce of appreciation in comparison with her. Yet he does more than uphold her as an unlikely example of humility and respectfulness. He connects the depth of her love to the depth of her need, saying to her, in full view of everyone present, "Your sins are forgiven" (7:48). Those are the most pressing words he has for her, the message of ultimate importance.

This shocks those in attendance even more than the woman's actions. "Who is this who even forgives sins?" they ask (7:49). The implication, spelled out elsewhere, is that only God has authority to forgive sins. The dinner guests, you see, know that forgiveness is essentially divine. Jesus is claiming to be not only God but the God whose forgiveness zeroes in on those who cannot hide the scars of a shame-filled past.

For the same reason—and I cannot stress this enough—it is imperative we take care in distinguishing between the command to forgive and the proclamation that, on account of Christ, you and I *are* forgiven. To exhort someone to forgive their enemies may be morally laudable, but it is not a relief, not when you are truly injured. In such cases, the command to forgive is received as a burden, sometimes a grave one. The truth is, you may not be able to forgive that person, and the relief comes in leaving such matters to God, who is not you. Meanwhile, after hearing that you've been forgiven by God, even for your grudge-holding inability to forgive, well, tears of gratitude might not be an overreaction.

Because God understands the fickleness of our hearts, he has grounded forgiveness outside the shifting sands of human resolve and in the death and resurrection of Christ. This is why Christians are bold enough to claim that God forgives *before* we have the chance to come clean (Rom. 5:8). That happy news may even give us the courage to realize just how much we need to do so.

Airborne Absolution

The late pastor and theologian Jim Nestingen made a career out of proclaiming God's forgiveness in its most radical expression. He told one story that I will never shake. It occurred during a period of his life when he was logging a lot of time at fifty thousand feet, traveling to speak at conferences all over the country. Jim, you should know, was a large man of Scandinavian stock, six feet five, and let's just say his lifelong appreciation of the Nordic beer-brewing tradition had left its mark.

Because of his size, Jim was not a fan of planes, particularly not of coast-to-coast flights. After shoehorning himself into a window seat one day, a man of similar dimensions sat down next to him. "There we were," Jim says, "like two heads on a pimple."

Since they were practically on top of each other, the two men began talking. His seatmate asked what Jim did for a living, and Jim said he was a preacher of the gospel. "Almost as soon as I got the words out, he shouted back at me over the plane's take-off noise: 'I'm not a believer!'"

But the man was curious, so once they reached cruising altitude, he asked Jim what it was like being a preacher. "After a bit, he says to me again: 'I'm not a believer.' So I say to him: 'Okay, but it doesn't change anything—he's already gone and done it all for you whether you like it or not.'"

The man then went quiet for a bit. When he started talking again, in what felt apropos of nothing, he proceeded to tell Jim stories about the Vietnam War. He had served as an infantryman in some of that conflict's bloodiest battles—Khe Sanh, the Tet Offensive, Hamburger Hill. "I did terrible things for my country," the man said. "And when I came home my country didn't want me to talk about it. I've had a terrible time living with it, living with myself."

This went on the whole flight, the man unloading all the awful things he'd seen and done. As they approached their destination, Jim asked, "Have you confessed all the sins now that have been troubling you?"

"What do you mean, confessed?! I've never confessed," the man replied.

"You've been confessing your sins to me this whole flight long," Jim said. "And I've been commanded by Christ Jesus that when I hear a confession like that to hand over the goods and speak a particular word to you. So, you have any more sins burdening you? If so, throw them in there."

"I'm done now," the man said. "I'm finished."

At this point he grabbed Jim's hand as though he'd just had a second thought. "But I told you—I'm not a believer. I don't have any faith in me."

Jim, however, was unbuckling his seatbelt and in the process of squeezing himself out of the row. "Well, that's quite all right, brother," he said. "Nobody has faith inside of them. Jesus says that what's inside of you is what's wrong with the world. I'm going to speak faith into you."

He stood up. The seatbelt sign had already dinged, though, and the tray tables were secured in their upright positions. The flight attendant noticed what was going on and started objecting: "Sir— *sir*—you can't do that. You must be seated immediately. You can't do that."

"Can't do it?" said Jim. "Ma'am, Christ our Lord commands me to do it."

She gave him a fearful look, worried that he might evangelize her next. The other passengers were going bananas. Jim ignored them all, turning to his neighbor and putting a hand on the man's head. "In the name of Jesus Christ and by his authority, I declare the entire forgiveness of all your sins."

"You—you can't do that," the man whispered.

"I *can* do it. I must. Christ compels me to do it. I just did it and I'll do it again."

He then did, loud enough for everyone on that plane to hear: "In the name of Jesus Christ and by his authority, I declare unto you the entire forgiveness of all your sins."

41

The man started sobbing uncontrollably, his shirt soon soaked from the tears. Jim sat down and put his arms around the man, the way one would around an inconsolable child. The flight attendant and all the rest who'd been fussing went silent. They seemed to recognize that something holy was happening in front of them.

As the plane was landing, the man gathered himself enough to ask Jim to absolve him again, and Jim obliged, repeating the same words. The man laughed and wiped his eyes and said, "Gosh, if that's true, it's the best news I've ever heard. I just can't believe it. It would take a miracle for me to believe something so crazy good."

Jim just chuckled. "Yep, it takes a miracle for all of us. It takes a miracle for every last one of us."

If that were the end of story, it would be a doozy. But as both men were retrieving their bags from the overhead compartment, Jim pulled his card out and handed it to his seatmate. "You're likely not going to believe your forgiveness tomorrow or the next day or a week from now. When you stop having faith in it, call me and I'll bear witness to you all over again. I'll keep on doing it until you do—you really do—trust and believe it."

From that day forward, the man called Jim every day to hear him declare the forgiveness of the gospel. "It got to be he couldn't live without it," Jim says. "And I bore witness to him every day right up to the day he died. I told him: In the name of Christ Jesus, I forgive you all your sins. I wanted the last words he heard in this life to be the first words he would hear Jesus himself say to him in the next life."[16]

Notice Jim didn't say, "I feel your pain." Nor did he attempt to rationalize it by saying something like, "Well, you were just doing your duty; don't be so hard on yourself." Jim also didn't dismiss the man's sin as the result of PTSD or deflect and try to take it on himself. No, Jim offered him the medicine of absolution. Like that library president in New York, he understood his vocation well. He

---

16. I came across this story in a pamphlet by author and pastor Jason Micheli. It is adapted and used with his permission.

knew he wasn't in the business of policing sins but in the business of bearing witness to God's forgiveness.

What that man on the plane experienced was the Big Relief of the gospel, which is the message that your sins are forgiven, your shame dispelled, your record expunged, your privileges reinstated. You don't have to hide your past anymore—or your crumbling library books. You can return them without fear of penalty. You can even crack them open.

3

Favor

The Relief from Rejection

"It's a lock," they told me. The team would meet for its annual post-season banquet. We'd eat some pizza, our coach would hand out a few awards, and then we'd elect next year's captains. I say captains, plural. My sophomore year there had been three. My junior year, two.

Water polo is what you call a niche sport—in New England at least. Sunny places like California and Florida boast robust high school water polo leagues, in both public and prep schools. These states tend to feed the US Olympic roster. In Connecticut, the sport is mainly something for swimmers to do during the offseason. No one takes it that seriously.

When I showed up at boarding school as a new sophomore, I had never played water polo before. I couldn't tell you the positions, certainly not the rules. I just knew there was a lot of treading water. The admissions office must have informed the coach of my facility in the pool, as he wasted no time urging me to go out for the team, assuring me that I'd have a leg up when swim season started that winter.[1]

---

1. This story is adapted, with permission, from my chapter, "Rejection and the Good News," in *The Jesus I Wish I Knew in High School*, ed. Cameron Cole and Charlotte Getz (New Growth, 2021), 78–82.

So out I went, kicking off three seasons of intense play. It turns out that being a good swimmer is more than half the battle. I wasn't going to make any all-American lists, but I more than held my own. By the end of that first year I was starting on varsity. The next fall, I was one of two juniors who started every game. The other was my good friend Myles.

This means that when captain elections came up, really only two guys were in the running. And since there had never been fewer than two captains, all that remained was to plan my acceptance speech. You can guess what happened next. The coach tallied the anonymous vote and announced that there would be just one captain next season, and it wouldn't be me.

I was dumbfounded. But this was no prank. Myles looked almost as shocked as I did. As the room emptied, everyone avoided eye contact with me, coach included. Writing about it now, I can still feel a knot form in my belly. The stakes may seem relatively minor, but the verdict cut to the core of my seventeen-year-old self.

Most rejections can be written off or minimized. We can appeal to the "Well, I didn't really try that hard" excuse or some form of "Who really cares?" In this case, I had tried my hardest for two full seasons. I had given everything I had and couldn't pretend I didn't care. The only way to interpret this rejection was as a public confirmation of every doubt I'd ever harbored about myself.[2] "You are no leader," my peers had effectively told me. "You do not have what it takes, and we will go out of our way to let you know that." I was devastated.

To this day, I have no idea what happened or why. The coach called me that evening but offered no explanation. He just wanted me to know that he could tell I was upset but hoped I would still get in the water next season. (Looking back, the nerve of this guy!)

The season after I graduated there would be two captains again, and to my knowledge there have been two every year since. Something

2. It's telling that I saw the opinion of my coach and teammates as authoritative. As far as I was concerned, theirs was the final word. The anger at myself would soon manifest as depression.

about me, I could only assume, was so noticeably not captain material that tradition had to be suspended. I ran into that coach when I was back for a reunion a decade later and remember fighting the urge to bring it up (or to kick him in the shins). These are the types of things you never forget; they can impact your sense of self-worth, or lack thereof, for years to come.

The pressure to belong—to be both loved *and* liked by others—is less of a pressure and more of a longing. I don't think it's an overstatement to say it shapes our lives from the moment we are born until the day we die. If we're fortunate, loving attachment to our parents and family meets this need for our first few years of life. As we grow older, we become our own person and detach, forming friendships and joining communities and pursuing romantic relationships, all in the hopes of belonging. The risk, at every stage, is rejection.

Perhaps *belonging* is too mild a word for what we're after. We want more than inclusion. We want welcome and warmth and, well, love. My spot on the water polo roster was secure, after all. What I was hoping for from my teammates was their approval and validation. I received the opposite. This rejection may not have involved expulsion, but the denial of favor sure felt like being cast out.

All the Lonely People

Rejection is so painful that we spend most of our lives avoiding it. When a friend or romantic partner rejects us, they're conveying a negative judgment about our worth. The result is separation, isolation, and loneliness. Of course, loneliness just as often arises from the fear of rejection as from rejection itself. Instead of submitting ourselves to the judgments of others, we keep a distance from them and accept loneliness as the cost for safety. Either way, loneliness is deadly.

Knowing other people and being known by them, it turns out, is vital to our well-being as humans. Study after study shows that the most reliable indicator of personal happiness has to do with the number and quality of our social connections. These studies also reveal the inverse. Social disconnection correlates to an increased risk of premature death comparable to smoking up to fifteen cigarettes every day.[3] Our risk of anxiety and depression rises when we are lonely, as does that of heart disease, dementia, and stroke.

The past few decades of life in the West have given researchers ample opportunity to study loneliness, as rates of self-reported loneliness have never been higher. In 2018 the United Kingdom appointed an official minister of loneliness, and in 2023 Surgeon General Vivek Murthy declared loneliness a public health epidemic on par with obesity.[4] Dr. Murthy cited a 2021 survey of more than two thousand adults in the United States, in which fewer than half the men said they were truly satisfied with how many friends they had, while 15 percent said they had no close friends at all—a fivefold increase since 1990.

It sometimes feels like contemporary society conspires to manufacture loneliness. The advent of remote work, for instance, forecloses one traditional avenue of interpersonal connection. Even if we do still go into the office, urban sprawl, lackluster mass transit, and ever burgeoning levels of traffic keep many of us in our cars, solo, for longer and longer portions of the day. I remember a few years ago reading an article lamenting the decrease in sleepovers among school-age children. Packed extracurricular schedules, combined with parental hypervigilance, mean that this beloved mainstay of my youth is going the way of the dodo.

Loneliness on this scale fosters a certain amount of pressure. That is, we put pressure on otherwise mundane activities to meet

3. Neha Kidambi and Ellen E. Lee, "Insight into Potential Mechanisms Linking Loneliness and Cognitive Decline: Commentary on 'Health Factors as Potential Mediators of the Longitudinal Effect of Loneliness on General Cognitive Ability,'" *National Library of Medicine* 28, no. 12 (August 2020): 1284–86, https://doi.org/10.1016/j.jagp.2020.08.015.

4. Office of the Surgeon General, "Our Epidemic of Loneliness and Isolation: The U.S. Surgeon General's Advisory on the Healing Effects of Social Connection and Community," U.S. Department of Health and Human Services, 2023, https://www.hhs.gov/sites/default/files/surgeon-general-social-connection-advisory.pdf.

our need for belonging, fashioning ersatz families out of whatever resources we have at hand. Thus, you see offices hiring spiritual consultants, mindfulness experts, and social coordinators to care for their employees. Gyms cease emphasizing fitness in their advertising and start emphasizing connection. Fan communities, from Swifties to Poké Fans, begin to function as de facto tribes, with their own shared story and language for people to inhabit together. Usually these sorts of affinity groups are benign and fun. Occasionally, as anyone who's attended a Philadelphia Eagles game knows, they get nasty.

The most popular road to belonging today is probably politics. The allure makes sense; when you share political commitments with others, you share not only values but also antagonisms. Nothing bonds people closer together—in the short run, at least—than a common enemy. If only such affiliations didn't play out predominantly online and absent of embodied community, then the belonging they offer might not be so thin. Even so, those who grew up in religious communities know that there's a dark side to politics-as-belonging. If we are leaning on a specific cause or ideology for social acceptance, then the *most* accepted will be those who espouse their views the loudest. Belovedness will be bestowed in proportion to the strength of our commitments. In such environments, hesitation and doubt become grounds for rejection, which incentivizes entrenchment, escalation, and even radicalization. In other words, when political arguments get overheated, it behooves those of us on the sidelines to remember that, for some people, it's not just policies at stake but personal acceptance.

In each of these cases, you'll notice that behavior precedes belonging. Entrance to the community depends on either doing something (well) or believing something (strongly)—or both.[5] Fellowship and favor are given according to whichever metric matters at the moment. Consciously or not, belovedness must be merited.

5. When the marketplace gets involved, which it often does, inclusion usually has a monetary fee associated with it too.

Eight Arms to Hold You

The Big Relief reverses the order of belonging. In a setting of grace, belonging precedes behavior. It comes first. Jesus often showed people favor before they made the smallest overture toward him. I think of the calling of his disciples James, John, Philip, and Nathanael. I think of the paralyzed man at the pool of Bethsaida (John 5). Most of all I think of a chief tax collector like Zacchaeus, whom Jesus approached and then invited himself to lunch with (Luke 19:1–10). Grace makes the first move.

Indeed, returning to John Barclay's book *Paul and the Gift*, recall that one of the key attributes of God's grace, according to Paul, is its priority. Paul asks, "Who has given a gift to [God] that he might be repaid?" And the answer is no one, for "from him and through him and to him are all things" (Rom. 11:35–36 ESV). Theologian Orrey McFarland writes, "Just as no one provoked God to create, so also no one provokes God to give: God's generosity happens prior to all human demands, claims, or worth."[6] This is immensely good news for those siloed in loneliness. I can't help but think of George McFly in the 1985 movie *Back to the Future*, a young man so petrified of rejection that he must be cajoled and ultimately threatened into inviting his future wife, Lorraine, to the Enchantment Under the Sea Dance. If it were up to him, he would never have made the first move. His time-traveling son, Marty, had to assure him of her favor before he was able to summon the nerve.

Grace is a relief to the lonely and rejected because it doesn't wait for us to drop our own walls. Grace breaks down, with love, the barriers we've erected to keep us safe in our isolation. Grace risks rejection itself. The other image that comes to mind in this respect involves the nonfictional enchantment under the sea depicted in the 2020 award-winning documentary *My Octopus Teacher*. On the surface, the film tells the story of filmmaker Craig Foster

6. Orrey McFarland, "The God Who Gives First," *Mockingbird*, October 14, 2020, https://mbird.com/bible/the-god-who-gives-first/.

and the touching relationship he develops with a local octopus. What it's really about, however, is Foster's journey back to the human race and to himself after years of estrangement.

The details of Foster's dislocation are never shared on camera; all we know is that, at the outset, he is suffering from burnout and a lack of purpose. In his malaise he has decided to return to the environs of his youth on the southernmost tip of South Africa, a place known as the Cape of Storms. Once there, he undertakes a daily free-diving regimen that revives his spirits. Each day he explores the freezing kelp forests off the coast, eventually discovering a female octopus that has made its den there. Foster is captivated by this alien creature and begins visiting the site daily, camera in hand. At first, he takes the stance of outward observer, not wanting to intrude on the octopus's habitat.

Then something unexpected happens. Despite the distance Foster keeps, the octopus gradually becomes less and less wary of him. Trust builds between man and animal until one day, while Foster is filming, the octopus reaches out its small tentacle and touches him on the finger. The octopus, of her own initiative, breaks the clinical barrier and connects with the human who's been hovering nearby. It's the turning point of Foster's life. This octopus was not content for him to be an impartial observer. She draws him in, and they develop the sort of relationship I didn't think would be possible.

For the final line of the film, Foster eulogizes his underwater friend, saying, "What she taught me was to feel that you're a part of this place, not a visitor. That is a huge difference." You can hear the emotion in his voice. Indeed, you can hear the relief. The octopus punctured Foster's isolation and welcomed him into her world. She refused to let him remain in his lonely exile. The priority of her action is what gives it such power.[7]

As the credits rolled, I thought of Jesus's immortal pronouncement in the Gospel of John: "You did not choose me, but I chose you" (15:16).

7. *My Octopus Teacher*, directed by Pippa Ehrlich and James Reed (Sea Change Project, 2020), Netflix, https://www.netflix.com/title/81045007.

Hug a Telemarketer

In the calculus of grace, belonging doesn't just precede behavior; it also targets misbehavior. When I worked as a youth minister, our go-to definition of *grace* was "unmerited favor." I liked that phrase then, and I like it now. It captures the revelation that God's favor extends precisely to those who have not merited it via their actions or convictions. "I have not come to call the righteous but sinners" is how Jesus puts it (Mark 2:17). This attitude caused immediate backlash for the way it inverted the usual order of things. "Why does he eat with tax collectors and sinners?" Jesus's onlookers grumbled (Mark 2:16).

From a spiritual and social point of view, Jesus favored the unfavorable. Sometimes these folks were marginalized because they were infirm or diseased, such as those suffering from leprosy. Sometimes they were ethnic or moral outcasts, as in the case of Samaritans and prostitutes. In such instances, modern sensibilities tend to locate a basis for sympathy. We can see why Jesus might grant such sufferers his attention. They didn't ask for their illness, after all. Their heritage—and whatever prejudices existed against it—wasn't elective. Even prostitution, we presume, must have been a last resort. In this way, we feel pity for those rejected by first-century society.

Yet if we're to grasp the radicality of grace, we must consider that some recipients of Jesus's favor were outcast for good reason. Tax collectors, for example, were essentially loan sharks who collaborated with an occupying government, oppressing their neighbors out of personal greed for the sake of the empire. *Reprehensible* is not too strong a word. Nevertheless, Jesus goes out of his way to spend time with them, choosing a tax collector named Matthew to be one his first disciples (Matt. 9:9–13). Later he breaks bread with Zacchaeus, and then, in one of his most famous parables, Jesus portrays a fictional tax collector favorably and a religious leader unfavorably (Luke 18:9–19:10).

What sort of people in our everyday lives do we universally despise without feeling bad for doing so, apart from archetypal bad guys like Nazis or Klan members? "Stage parents"—those overambitious moms and dads who go to any length to get their kid on-screen when they're young—strike me as a pretty unlovable demographic. Maybe that's more of a personal peeve, though. A generous soul might say the parents' only crime is loving their kids too much. Same goes, I guess, for those appalling guys who get in fistfights on the sidelines of Little League games. Several years ago, the internet decided that Karens and Kyles were the worst, but there's a generational element to those resentments that keeps them from being universal. Plus, I know some wonderful ladies named Karen.[8] More recently, "Disney adults"—that is, grown-up Mickey Mouse superfans who visit the company's theme parks without kids in tow—were deemed the creepiest subset of the population. Of course, those of us with active inner children beg to differ.

Then it hit me: no group is more casually hateable than telemarketers. To be clear, I'm not talking about folks who voluntarily make calls to raise money or awareness for a cause they believe in—or, really, those who want us to switch insurance companies (in the middle of dinner). I'm talking about a specific type of tele- or e-marketer. Call them spammers or catfishers or gift-card grifters; they make a living by preying on the elderly, the unaware, and those for whom English is a second language. Every pastor I know has a story of their church database getting hacked and their congregants receiving phony emails or texts, under the clergy's name, asking for emergency funds.[9] When I need to picture someone irredeemable, that's where my brain goes.[10]

I'm trying to conjure up a sense of "acceptable" contempt and am probably making it harder than it has to be. We live, after all, in what some commentators have termed a "culture of contempt."[11] If anger

8. Kyles, on the other hand . . .
9. Those who open their wallets in response tend to be the sweetest and most guileless members, which only compounds the ugliness at work.
10. Spend much time in an eldercare facility, and the stories you hear will make your skin crawl. I heard one about a nonagenarian almost giving $30,000 of their savings to a perfect stranger who had called them under false pretenses. A special circle of hell, my friends.
11. Arthur C. Brooks, "Our Culture of Contempt," *New York Times*, March 2, 2019, https://www.nytimes.com/2019/03/02/opinion/sunday/political-polarization.html.

is an evaluation of someone's actions, contempt is an evaluation of someone's value. Think of contempt as anger plus disgust. According to nineteenth-century philosopher Arthur Schopenhauer, contempt is "the unsullied conviction of the worthlessness of another."[12] If you have contempt for someone, then, you believe they are beneath caring about. In his book *Love Your Enemies*, Arthur Brooks diagnoses Americans as addicted to political contempt in particular.[13]

No word better describes those we hold in contempt than *enemy*. Your enemy, by definition, exists beyond the limits of sympathy. If that term is too bold for you, though, think about how we use the word *toxic* these days. When I first heard it used in relation to people, *toxic* was invoked to describe a leader who was fostering a demoralizing culture in their area of influence. The term struck me as a smart way of describing someone who has a manipulative and egomaniacal style of relating and who, by virtue of their authority, has infected the community in their care with suspicion and blame. Doublespeak, backbiting, and even harassment are hallmarks of toxic workplaces, and if you've ever had the misfortune of being employed at one, you know that *toxic* is an apt term. The ugliness you experience nine-to-five can have a cancerous effect on the rest of your life. Positions of power often seem to cater to toxic individuals. Or maybe power itself is toxifying—I don't know.[14]

What I do know is that the scope of the word has crept outward to include more than just those in authority. I recently heard a fellow parent refer to one of my son's fifth-grade classmates as toxic.[15] It's not uncommon to classify former friends (or ex-BFFs) as toxic. Of course, no one ever describes themselves this way; we reserve the term for our, well, enemies. Perhaps we do this because there's something mildly

12. Arthur Schopenhauer, "On Religion: A Dialogue," in *The Horrors and Absurdities of Religion*, trans. R. J. Hollingdale (Penguin, 1970), 11.

13. Arthur C. Brooks, *Love Your Enemies: How Decent People Can Save America from the Culture of Contempt* (HarperCollins, 2019), 28.

14. Sadly, in twenty-plus years of experience in church and church-adjacent settings, I've run into more than my fair share of toxic leaders. That ecclesial structures would attract such folks makes sense—they're accessible spheres of influence over vulnerable people. That the church would enable, and sometimes reward, such behavior makes less sense. It's the definition of *tragic*.

15. And I heard myself agree!

absolving about the word. It allows us to perceive our enemies less as adversaries to be defeated or folks we're in conflict with and more as defiling influences to be purged. Journalist Kaitlyn Tiffany writes,

> The internet is wallpapered with advice, much of it delivered in a cut-and-dried, cut-'em-loose tone. Frankly worded listicles abound. For instance: "7 Tips for Eliminating Toxic People From Your Life," or "7 Ways to Cut a Toxic Friend Out of Your Life." On Instagram and Pinterest, the mantras are ruthless: "There is no better self-care than cutting off people who are toxic for you"; "If I cut you off, chances are, you handed me the scissors." . . . *I don't know who needs to hear this*, a tweet will begin, suggesting that almost anyone might need to hear it, *but if someone hurts your feelings, you are allowed to get rid of them.*[16]

Enemies should not be coddled or endured, in other words. They should be excised and eliminated. Again, this assumes that no one thinks of *us* in this way.

Much as I sometimes wish it weren't the case, Jesus is not on board with the vanquishing of one's enemies. He does not endorse repaying enmity with enmity. Revenge is wholly foreign to his way of thinking. Instead, he suggests that grace exceeds the bounds of affinity. Love, for it to be the type that Jesus advocates, extends favor to your worst nightmare. In Luke 6:27–36 he says,

> But I say to you who are listening: Love your enemies; do good to those who hate you; bless those who curse you; pray for those who mistreat you. If anyone strikes you on the cheek, offer the other also, and from anyone who takes away your coat do not withhold even your shirt. . . .
>
> If you love those who love you, what credit is that to you? For even sinners love those who love them. . . . Instead, love your enemies, do good, and lend, expecting nothing in return. Your reward will be great,

16. Kaitlyn Tiffany, "That's It. You're Dead to Me," *Atlantic*, August 13, 2022, https://www.theatlantic.com/magazine/archive/2022/09/toxic-person-tiktok-internet-slang-meaning/670599/ (emphasis in original).

and you will be children of the Most High, for he himself is kind to the ungrateful and the wicked.

Notice that Jesus does not say "tolerate your enemies" or "gently correct your ideological opponents" or even "be nice to bullies in the hopes of them becoming friends." He exhorts us to lovingly seek our enemies' good and not to expect anything in return—not reward or thanks or apology. It is worth clarifying that lovingly seeking our enemy's good is not the same as enabling them. Love may mean removing ourselves from their sphere of influence for a while—or for good. It may mean protecting our enemy from their worst inclinations via a confrontation of some kind. It could take any number of forms. But love never exonerates or encourages abuse; that wouldn't be loving to the victim *or* the abuser. We can seek our enemy's good through prayer without ever having to see them again.

The world may cast such a view as an invitation to doormat city, but I wonder if it's actually an invitation to hope. After all, no parent ever won their estranged child back through criticism. Consequences (of our own devising) seldom engender reconciliation. "Love to the loveless shown," as the old hymn puts it, is the only thing that can do the trick.[17] It is certainly the only thing that did the trick when *we* were on the other side of the equation, which we all will be at some point or other.

Unreasonable Hospitality

Another euphemism I like for *grace* is the one coined by restaurateur Will Guidara in the title of his book *Unreasonable Hospitality*. Guidara started out his career working for culinary superstar Danny Meyer in New York City, taking over as general manager of Meyer's Eleven Madison Park in 2006. In 2011 Guidara, along with chef Daniel Humm, purchased the restaurant from Meyer's group.

17. "My Song Is Love Unknown," by Samuel Crossman, 1664.

Then, in 2017, the duo shocked gourmets around the globe when Eleven Madison Park topped the World's 50 Best Restaurants list. In his book, Guidara outlines the philosophy that guided their meteoric rise, highlighting a few of the hospitality maxims that Meyer imparted to all his employees: "My favorite was 'make the charitable assumption,' a reminder to assume the best of people, even when (or perhaps especially when) they weren't behaving particularly well. . . . When someone is being difficult, it's human nature to decide they no longer deserve your best service. But another approach is to think, 'Maybe the person is being dismissive because their spouse asked for a divorce or because a loved one is ill. Maybe this person needs more love and more hospitality than anyone else in the room.'"[18]

If this sounds a bit like the noncomplementary behavior described in chapter 1, or the mitigation that often precedes forgiveness in chapter 2, that's not a coincidence. Meyer, and by extension Guidara, is advocating for something supremely counterintuitive: that restaurant (and hotel) staff lavish their customers with courtesy and kindness even and especially when their behavior deserves censure. When the guest is acting most unfavorably is when you pour on the favor. As the title suggests, nothing is reasonable about this policy. On the surface it may even appear that the restaurant and its staff are allowing themselves to be disrespected—or taken advantage of.

But grace is never reasonable. There is little difference, in practice, between such a policy and how God treats you and me at our most toxic moments. God doesn't just refuse to push us away or to cut us off; he brings us closer. The main difference is that no money changes hands. In fact, if there's a bill involved, the manager foots it.

Many an unruly diner has doubtless been soothed by an extra dessert on the house. Still, the servers I've spoken to always have a story of that one table that resists every extension of hospitality: the guest who has had far too much to drink or far too little sleep or is simply out for blood and nothing will placate them. It is an

---

18. Will Guidara, *Unreasonable Hospitality: The Remarkable Power of Giving People More Than They Expect* (Penguin Random House, 2022), 29.

incontrovertible truth of human nature that sick people often balk at healing. Part of the curse of loneliness is that it can inspire us to batten down the hatches and repel anyone who tries to come near.

Fortunately, "love your enemies" isn't just an ethic Jesus proclaims but one he embraces. Jesus did not and does not dole out favor in accordance with who is good or pure or enemy-less. He takes his cue instead from "the Most High," who "is kind to the ungrateful and the wicked" (Luke 6:35). That is, Jesus doles out kindness to the enemies of God, repaying scorn with mercy, contempt with amnesty, and toxicity with redemption. He doles out the Big Relief.

Remember, Jesus was rejected by his closest disciples—his teammates, if you will—but did not reject them in return. Instead, he took on the full weight of their negativity (and thirst for glory) and allowed it to crush him.

This means that the voices that echo through the halls of every high school, and sometimes in our own heads, are different from the voice of God. God's approval of you is not subject to any vote or public opinion. It is subject only to the grace of the one true Captain himself. The rejection we fear—indeed, the rejection we may experience from our peers or from the authority figures in our lives—is not the rejection of God.

The cross constitutes God's refusal to reject those who have rejected him. As Paul writes in 2 Corinthians, "As surely as God is faithful, our word to you has not been 'Yes and No.' For the Son of God, Jesus Christ, whom we proclaimed among you, Silvanus and Timothy and I, was not 'Yes and No,' but in him it has always been 'Yes.' For in him every one of God's promises is a 'Yes'" (1:18–20). In other words, for every banquet that goes disastrously wrong in this life, there is one in the next life that will not disappoint, where every tearful rejection will be made right.

I spoke with my old teammate Myles—you remember, *Captain Myles*—on the phone not long ago, and we both agreed that I would've made an insufferable captain. Fortunately, God favored me enough to save me from what I wanted. He will save you too. It's a lock.

4

Surrender

The Relief from Control

Of all the personality types we throw around today, one is more ubiquitous than the rest. Drop your Enneagram number into casual conversation, and only a few folks will have a frame of reference. Mention your Myers-Briggs type, and a couple more may know what you're talking about. But describe another person as "really type A," and odds are you won't need to extrapolate. That person is a go-getter, a leader: driven, high-energy, assertive, not what you'd call "chill."

The A-B distinction was coined in the mid-1970s by two cardiologists, Meyer Friedman and Ray Rosenman, to characterize the patients on their operating tables. By their estimation, so-called Alphas tended to lead more stressful lives, putting them at greater risk of heart disease. Those they termed "Betas" exhibited more laid-back dispositions and thus went easier on their arteries. Alphas, they claimed, were anxious, ambitious, and high-strung. Betas were laissez-faire and accommodating.[1] The distinction was an anecdotal one and does not hold up to scientific scrutiny, not that it really needs to.

---

1. Arlin James Benjamin Jr., "Type A/B Personalities," *The Wiley Encyclopedia of Personality and Individual Differences*, 4 vols. (John Wiley & Sons, 2020), 4:383–86.

Certainly, we live in a type-A culture. Entrepreneurs, not poets, are our heroes these days. Initiative as opposed to, say, patience is the virtue we emphasize to young people. "Stop waiting; start living," we tell one another. If you want to get ahead, you've got to be a self-starter. You can sleep when you're dead. #YOLO.

The message is clear: activity is preferable to passivity. That is, the A-B distinction carries moral weight. Type B-ness equates to resignation, unseriousness, and possibly even laziness. Type As, on the other hand, get things done. They are forces to be reckoned with. The world needs more doers, less spectators. Type Bs may be easier to get along with, but that's just because they're more malleable, less substantial. To be active is to exert one's power and control over the world around you. To be passive is to abdicate that control to others.

The pressure that a type-A world exerts on all of us, whether we buy into the dichotomy or not, is the pressure to be in control of everything, all the time. The goal of life, we presume, is dominion. Blessed are they who are in control of their schedule, their career, their children, and their future.

Yet as much as our advertising and self-help literature perpetuate this pressure, it does not derive from "out there." We only live in a type-A world because you and I have made it that way. Part of being an inheritor of what the Bible calls sin is that we compulsively grasp for (and hoard) power that is not ours to wield. Refusing divine authority and believing that we know best—this is the drama that we see played out from the beginning, starting in the garden of Eden. It was disastrous then, and it is disastrous now. Our hands are simply not big enough to hold the reins, and our muscles are too weak to steer the ship. The burden of control is beyond human capacity.

Ctrl-Alt-Delete

Consider the ways we try to control other people. We get scared that someone will hurt us, so we clamp down and try to influence their actions and thoughts such that their will does not depart from our own. Sadly, relationships where one person controls the other—through manipulation or guilt or violence—tend to be abusive ones. And even when that leverage takes a milder form, closeness is never the result. Our controlling actions are experienced as distrust by the person we are trying to impel to this or that end. Our anxiety pushes them away and makes us both feel more alone.

Maybe you find yourself in a relationship with a parent or significant other whose overreach has grown stifling. There may have been a time when their behavior felt nurturing. They cared enough to help and protect you; you were happy to follow their direction. Sadly, these patterns have a way of souring as the relationship goes on. When we cede our sense of self to an overbearing individual—or when they prove incapable of pulling back when we no longer need them so acutely—rebellion (or shutdown) is a foregone conclusion. Interpersonal control produces resentment, not intimacy.

People and circumstances aren't the only things we try to control. When something eventful happens in our lives, we often seek to "control the narrative," a euphemism for shaping the story that gets told about the events in question, and thereby the public perception. At 10:00 a.m. a politician gets caught with their hand in the campaign funds till, and by 11:00 they have issued a statement positioning their actions as defensible and even noble. A couple files for divorce, and, before the settlements have been signed, each partner has done their best to paint the breakup in the most flattering light possible. History is written by the victors, right?

The most common way we control the narrative is through the story we tell the world about ourselves. This can be as overt as the highlight reel of vacation pics we post to social media, or it can be as subtle as the facts we omit from our résumé. Perhaps we construct a public facade for ourselves, editing our personalities and neurotically monitoring our every utterance, such that nothing is left to chance when it comes to what others think of us. Whatever the case, we are attempting to control how others perceive us, and it is as exhausting as it is isolating. A world of type As frantically trying to control every outcome is a worn-out world.

And yet, the urge to exert a measure of agency over our own lives is not necessarily a dictatorial one. In fact, it is very difficult—impossible even—to live well without some degree of power over one's life.[2] Robbing others of their locus of control is more than just demoralizing; it is enslaving. HBO Sports once did a segment on Will Shortz, the man in charge of the *New York Times* crossword puzzles. He is a bit of a god among those who enjoy brainteasers. During the interview, Shortz was asked why he thinks people like puzzles so much: "The fascination is feeling in control. So much of life we have no control over. We just muddle through our private problems and move on to the next thing. With a crossword, or other human-made puzzle, you have achieved perfection. That's very satisfying."[3]

Puzzles, in other words, have right answers and wrong answers, and that clarity can be a relief in a world of "muddling through." Wordle is satisfying because of how its solvability represents a reprieve from the reality we occupy every other hour of the day. It gives us a healthy sense of control.[4] The problem, as Shortz hints, is that this control, and the peace it brings, will always be short-lived. Human beings simply do not possess the power sufficient to subjugate our environment on anything more than a provisional basis. Complete mastery is unavailable to limited people, and to pretend otherwise is a recipe for defeat, bitterness, and even madness.

If you don't believe me, try raising a child.

But there's a deeper problem with control as the be-all and end-all of existence: that which we use to control our lives often ends up controlling us.[5]

2. Jonathan Haidt, "Why the Mental Health of Liberal Girls Sank First and Fastest," *After Babel*, March 9, 2023, https://www.afterbabel.com/p/mental-health-liberal-girls.
3. "Will Shortz and the Puzzling Sport of Crosswords (Full Segment)," excerpt from *Real Sports with Bryant Gumbel*, interview, posted by HBO, May 24, 2018, YouTube, https://www.youtube.com/watch?v=GcKFU8BPJnc.
4. Except those days when it makes us feel profoundly stupid. I'm looking at you, *tacit*.
5. We'll explore this theme further, through the lens of captivity (and addiction), in the final chapter.

The Mystique of Technique

Probably the most well-known advertising maxim is Sex Sells. The idea is that if you want folks to buy your salad dressing, make sure the people consuming it in your commercial are extremely attractive.[6] Making a connection to the bedroom is a safe bet when moving product.

I think Control Sells is even safer. Peruse the internet or simply talk to peers at a dinner party, and you'll hear about new ways to consolidate your energy, optimize your efficiency, organize your priorities, maximize your property value, and make your life more *manageable*. The marketplace inundates us with formulas and fixes that promise, along with happiness, increased control.

French sociologist Jacques Ellul uses the term *technique* to describe our obsession with streamlining everything under the sun. He defines it as "the totality of methods rationally arrived at and having absolute efficiency (for a given stage of development) in every field of human activity."[7] Technique aims to bring efficiency to everything in life. Anytime we use machine logic and apply it to humanity, we are in the realm of technique. For example, we don't refine our morning routine so much as "hack" it. We don't make the most of our vacation; we "optimize" it. Technique is so ingrained in our day-to-day that we hardly notice it.

There's nothing wrong with conserving our time and resources, of course, or with wanting our lives to run more smoothly. What's wrong, Ellul believes, is that technique doesn't actually accomplish these goals. Technique promises to make life more convenient, affordable, and easy but in practice makes it more tiring, expensive, and complicated. Each new technique we adopt for the sake of greater control creates problems for which we instinctually look for another technique to allay, and so on.

6. Not a hypothetical. The commercials that Kraft put together for its "zesty" salad dressing line in 2013 resemble Harlequin romance book covers.
7. Jacques Ellul, *The Technological Society*, trans. John Wilkinson (Vintage, 1964), xxv.

Most children today are required to have laptop computers to do their schoolwork. A lot of schools go so far as to issue them to the kids. In theory, the technology is supposed to make the process of communication between teachers and students more seamless. Rather than print out an assignment and hand it to your teacher, you click a button to turn it in. Yet somehow I spend as much time troubleshooting the various homework programs on my sons' computers, updating software, and filling out endless two-factor authentications, as I do helping them with their homework. Once I had finally gotten it set at the end of last year, the school system moved to a newer and better program. It is a crazy-making experience that leaves everyone frustrated, tired, and not remotely in the mood for learning. No wonder the market for pillows—nay, the entire sleep industry!—is exploding. We need relief.

Some would characterize religion as a mammoth attempt to impose order on the chaos of life. Perhaps you've met someone who views God as a means to achieve such and such desired result in their life, whether that be happiness or prosperity or equity. Anytime someone is handing out a road map to guaranteed sanctification along a reliable timeline, you are in the realm of technique. Unfortunately, when churches bed down in technique, they do so at the expense of the Big Relief. After all, a god who is subject to our control is no god at all. Furthermore, the language of efficiency is foreign to Jesus. His time management was abysmal; he did not make strategic use of the resources at his disposal. If he was trying to control people, he did a poor job of it; the movement around him dwindled while he was alive, and in the end all his disciples bailed. Jesus Christ was clearly not a type-A personality.

Blessed Are the Type Bs

The human obsession with control was nonetheless alive and well in Jesus's time. What did the Romans value if not mastery at all costs? Yet Jesus seemed notably uninterested in playing the empire game. He saw through its allure, heaping the majority of his attention on people who had *lost* control over their lives (if they had it in the first place): the poor and powerless, the sick and marginalized, and all those who couldn't bootstrap themselves into righteousness.

Moreover, in his ministry Jesus did not introduce new or improved technique. He endorsed its opposite—namely, the grace of surrender. Take the healing of the paralyzed man in Mark 2. Jesus enters the town of Capernaum, and his reputation is already such that, when he stops to teach, the assembled crowd is so thick in the room that no one can get close to him. This presents a problem for the four men who have lugged their paralyzed friend to the venue in hopes that Jesus might heal him. With no other option, they decide to climb onto the roof and dismantle a person-sized portion of it so that they can lower their friend down. Jesus does not castigate the men or make a fuss about the destroyed property. He sees their faith and responds by first forgiving the paralyzed man his sins and then healing him.

The funereal imagery is not lost on psychologist Frank Lake, who writes, "[The paralyzed man] had been condemned by his illness to a passivity that overcame his contradictory and self-destructive drives. Thus the paralytic was lowered, like a dead body into a grave. The priest, Jesus himself, is waiting for the 'corpse,' not at the graveside, but at the bottom of it."[8]

The paralyzed man does not contribute to or cooperate with the cure that Jesus enacts. He was neither an instigator nor collaborator. Jesus may have smiled on the faith of the pallbearers, but they were not the recipients of the healing; the entirely passive man on the stretcher was. In fact, had Jesus appealed to the man's agency, the entreaty would have been absurd to the point of cruelty. The paralyzed man's nervous system exempted him from the world of technique, though thankfully not from the love of his friends.

Passivity served as a precondition for redemption. The same was true for the blind man at the pool of Siloam (John 9) and Jairus's

8. Frank Lake, as quoted in Ethan Richardson, "Condemned by Illness to Passivity," *Mockingbird*, June 9, 2016, https://mbird.com/theology/condemned-by-illness-to-passivity/.

daughter (Mark 5). Elsewhere, Jesus chastised the overactive Martha and praised her more type-B sister, Mary (Luke 10). These episodes suggest that our endless activity may, in fact, be a problem when it comes to experiencing healing, goodness, and God.

The Big Relief is not merely that God can and does act where human control fails but that God moves into those places with grace. In the preface to his commentary on Galatians, Martin Luther draws out this theme. Luther lists a few different forms of "active" righteousness—civil, cultural, ethical—before subordinating them all to that type of righteousness the paralyzed man encounters. Here is how the late pastor Tim Keller paraphrases Luther:

> There is another, a far better righteousness, which Paul calls "the righteousness of faith"—Christian righteousness. The other kinds of righteousness we can work at ourselves, by our own strength. But this Christian righteousness is the greatest of all. God puts it on us without our lifting a finger. It has nothing to do with obeying God's law; it has nothing to do with what we do or how hard we work, but it is given to us and we do nothing for it. It is a passive righteousness, while the others we have to work for. . . . And it is free righteousness, for we don't do anything or give anything to God to get it, but receive it, because someone else has done all the work for it in our place. . . . Nothing gives peace like this passive righteousness.[9]

Jesus wanted his followers to give up on trying to engineer their own security and well-being because he knew that only then would they put their faith in God rather than technique. Only then would self-confidence be supplanted by what Alcoholics Anonymous calls "God-confidence." Sometimes the only way to turn a type-A achiever into a type-B receiver is to inspire a nervous breakdown.

9. Timothy J. Keller, *The Message of Romans: Leader's Guide* (Redeemer Presbyterian Church, 2003), 8, https://graceb3.s3.amazonaws.com/wp-content/uploads/2018/05/Romans -Leaders-Guide-1.pdf (emphasis removed). Keller abridges and adapts Luther's words in this study guide.

It's a Pirate's Life for Me

Nervous breakdowns are not talked about as much as they used to be.[10] We speak instead today of meltdowns, panic attacks, breaks with reality, total freak-outs, and so on. Perhaps that's because the phrase *nervous breakdown* feels a bit antiquated. For me it conjures up the image of an otherwise buttoned-up 1950s housewife taking to the backyard with a shotgun to sniper some geese, à la Betty Draper in *Mad Men*.

What's nice about the language of *nervous breakdown* is how it allows for a person to snap without pathologizing the experience. It doesn't automatically connote mental illness. The term acknowledges that life on earth is sufficiently arduous that, every so often, we reach the limit of what we can deal with and can go no further. *Nervous breakdown* describes the collapse that ensues when we reach the end of our sense of control. It names what happens when we can no longer keep it together. Such breakdowns often double as breakthroughs—at least to the extent that they double as experiences of surrender. In this sense, they tend to represent the action of grace in the lives of control freaks like you and me.

The television show *Parenthood* provides a touching illustration of what this looks like. Loosely adapted from the film of the same name starring Steve Martin, the show aired from 2010 to 2016, chronicling the ups and downs of the extended Braverman family in Berkeley, California.[11] At the beginning of the first season, middle-aged parents Adam and Kristina Braverman realize that something is amiss with their son, Max. His stubbornness exceeds that of a kid being a kid, and his compulsiveness starts to concern them. The presenting symptom is Max's refusal to dress in anything but a pirate costume. Adam, afraid that his son will get made fun of at school,

10. Jerry Useem, "Bring Back the Nervous Breakdown," *Atlantic*, February 8, 2021, https://www.theatlantic.com/magazine/archive/2021/03/bring-back-the-nervous-breakdown/617788/.

11. In many ways *Parenthood* was the "blue state" version of the showrunner Jason Katims's previous series, the exquisite *Friday Night Lights*.

finds himself increasingly exasperated. Over dinner one evening, Adam attempts to get Max to put away his pet cockroach and eat his meal—Max is very particular about his diet—going so far as to barter with him, offering more minutes of TV time for more bites of food. The tactic backfires, and the next scene finds Adam and Kristina lying in bed, unable to sleep.

A few days later, the Bravermans meet with the sought-after child psychologist Dr. Pelikan. The doctor informs Adam and Kristina that Max's behavior is consistent with Asperger's syndrome. They look like they've been hit in the face.

> Adam: How long is this going to take, then? To get him through this and back on track?
>
> Dr. Pelikan: Unfortunately there is no cure for Asperger's. It is a syndrome that he will always have.
>
> Adam: I don't understand.
>
> Kristina: What are we supposed to do for him? I don't know . . .
>
> Adam (clearly irritated): So just in case we can never see you again, what do you suggest we do to get him out of the pirate costume?
>
> Dr. Pelikan: The first step is not to wrench Max out of his comfort zone; the first step is to join Max where he is. And when he's ready, you walk him into the world.

Later, watching Max play outside in his pirate costume, Adam confesses, "Kristina, I just, I don't . . . I can deal with anything. I can deal with disease, with illness, with a broken bone. Give me something I can fix. But I don't know how to deal with this. This is for life." It is a powerful admission of helplessness. Having reached the point of defeat, there is only one thing left for Adam to do. He surrenders. A few scenes later, we watch as Adam, dressed from head to toe in his own pirate outfit, joins Max in the backyard. They run and jump and joust with their tennis racquets as the light fades, laughter filling their home for the first time in ages. While Paul Simon's "St. Judy's Comet" plays, Kristina stands in the doorway with a cup of tea in her hand, a hopeful smile dawning on her face.[12]

The show paints a picture of a neurodivergent child with whom conventional strategies of parental control fail. Rules, rewards, bargaining, punishment, and so forth find no foothold with Max, either behaviorally or motivationally. Adam and Kristina stumble on a different approach but only after the painful process of acceptance. Grace is born of the abandonment of control.

Yet grace is not a new or better technique; it is what happens when technique fails. Grace is not just another way to control a person. The moment someone surrenders their agenda for us and gives us the space to be ourselves, the sensation is close to that of love. When someone approaches us with curiosity rather than technique, we tend to feel safe and valued and only want to spend more time in their company.

Occasionally, perhaps, we are given to love others in this way, and it is a beautiful thing. When it comes to God, however, we would do well to remember that we are the Max in the equation, not the Adam. We are the child, not the parent. Or, we arrrrrrr the child, as the case may be.

Pray for a Nervous Breakdown

What the Christian faith has to offer the world, in lieu of another formula or life hack, is the hope of surrender. Surrender is hopeful because where human control ends, faith in God begins. This is not faith-for-faith's-sake but faith in the God who creates something out of nothing and brings resurrection out of crucifixion. Come to find out, the opposite of faith isn't doubt but control. This means that if life feels like a nonstop assault on your sense of control, then not only are you well within the mainstream of the human race, but you

---

12. *Parenthood*, season 1, episode 1, "Pilot," directed by Thomas Schlamme, written by Jason Katims, Ron Howard, and Lowell Ganz, aired March 2, 2010, on NBC.

may also be in the throes of the Big Relief. No matter how painful the breakdown feels, something is happening that technique could never accomplish.

I asked my mother once what she wished she'd have known as a young parent and if she had any guidance for my wife and me as we navigated that stage ourselves. She said something I'll never forget: "My chief prayer for my children has always been that they would have their nervous breakdown early, and with as little damage as possible." When I asked her to elaborate, she made it clear she wasn't praying for her kids to suffer pain; nor was she praying that we would experience diagnosable mental anguish. Of course not. She was praying that her boys would come into contact with their own limitations sooner rather than later, such that they might reach out for "a power greater than themselves" before the stakes of such a meltdown were too high. She wanted us to have a relationship with God, and she knew that no number of parental lectures or Sunday school classes could make that happen, not in the same way that an honest and uncontrived encounter with the reality of a loving God could. Her prayers were answered, and I thank God for it.

This means that church is not a place to expand our agency by incorporating spiritual technique so much as a place to give it up. It is where we go—theoretically—to wave our white flag without threat of friendly fire. Surrender may be frightening, but to those type As who have been trying to white-knuckle their way through life, the invitation to let go often comes as an enormous relief. This is not a onetime thing either. Surrender, which Christians tend to refer to as "repentance," happens moment by moment. You might call it a way of life.

The breakdown-as-breakthrough dynamic syncs with an addiction model of spiritual growth, in which true recovery begins with a bottoming out. In her memoir, *Sober Mercies*, Heather Kopp discloses what happens when a successful writer/editor of Christian books and mother of two finds herself in rehab in midlife. About two-thirds of the way into the book, Heather describes a relapse.

She had long thought of herself as a sinner saved by grace, but only during this defeat, cowering in her closet, did she experience what those words mean:

> Up until that day when I fell on my knees and sobbed beside my bed, God's grace had been a nice option, a convenient option, but not my only option. . . . It was a painful epiphany with enormous implications. Among other things, it meant that if I was ever going to experience the kind of ongoing spiritual transformation I so desperately wanted, I would have to learn the difference between ascribing to a set of Christian beliefs that had no power to change me, and clinging daily to an experience of God's love and grace that could.[13]

Heather was given what people in recovery sometimes call the gift of desperation, and it formed the bedrock of her survival—to say nothing of her faith. Indeed, testimonies like this are a mainstay of twelve-step meetings, the first three steps of which, non-coincidentally, involve the admission of unmanageability and surrender to a higher power. This process can be painful to say the least, but only as a precursor to deep relief. Fortunately, the pattern holds in more formal religious circles. Conversion usually feels less like being convinced and more like acquiescence.

Advertise Your Hypocrisy

Two fruits of surrender are honesty and patience. Each flows from the blessed passivity at the heart of the gospel. First, the pronouncement of God's forgiveness and favor gives a person permission to abandon their attempts to manage other people's impressions twenty-four seven, whether that be through omission or deception or spin or what have you. Instead of expressing only those things about ourselves that we deem acceptable or admirable, grace frees us to try what one friend of mine calls "the ole telling-the-truth trick."

13. Heather Kopp, *Sober Mercies* (Hachette Book Group, 2014), 145.

This has less to do with flaunting weakness or airing dirty laundry than with no longer hiding. We can advertise our hypocrisy.

Hypocrisy, it's safe to say, is considered shameful. It is something to be diminished as much as possible, concealed, if not outright denied, a categorical no-no in pretty much every context I can think of. Hypocrisy is the basis for a great deal of our negative judgments of others and the substance of most "gotcha" attempts: "Can you believe he's sending his kid to private school after all those years haranguing us about the virtues of public education?" "Listen, you're free to spend your money however you want, but maybe don't lecture the rest of us about sacrifice from the front seat of your new Range Rover!"

Perhaps we believe that such a thing as a nonhypocrite exists—and that we have the option of being one. Alas, as Aldous Huxley writes, "The only completely consistent people are the dead."[14] The Big Relief brings with it the realization that we are all, to some extent, hypocritical. We have left undone those things that we ought to have done and vice versa. No one anywhere is living with full consistency. Instead of cloaking us in shame, however, acknowledging this builds commonality and lets us be more transparent with one another and ourselves.

When Jesus calls the Pharisees hypocrites, he is speaking to religious leaders who believe themselves not to be such (Matt. 23:27). He is indicting those who've bought into the myth of their own righteousness and are lording it over others. What he counsels them is the same thing he counsels us: to take the plank out of our own eyes before examining the speck in our neighbor's (Matt. 7). Jesus urges us, in other words, to give up our attempts at meticulously curating appearances for the sake of maximum approval from others and ultimately from God.

This is not the same thing as celebrating hypocrisy. That any of us betrays our convictions is not a proud thing. Saying one

14. Aldous Huxley, "Wordsworth in the Tropics," in *Do What You Will: Essays* (Chatto & Windus, 1929), 125.

thing and doing another causes real pain, both to others and to ourselves. A better world would be one in which integrity came easily to human beings. Advertising hypocrisy is simply leading with an admission of contradiction. It entails dropping the pretense of consistency from the outset and placing ourselves—or being placed—in the category of those Jesus came to save. There's freedom in this advertisement. It is the freedom to be a little less concerned with projecting a watertight persona to the world. That ship has sailed.

Contrary to the mobs we encounter on social media, though, hypocrisy does not disqualify a person from love, not the kind of love that Jesus spoke about and embodied with hypocrites like Peter. As trauma therapist Kobe Campbell puts it, "Healing is not becoming the best version of yourself; healing is letting the worst version of yourself be loved."[15]

To advertise our hypocrisy is to say to the world, "Come on in, there's room for one more. You don't have to pretend any longer to be something you're not and can never be. Belovedness is not contingent on your virtue—or even your honesty about your lack thereof." It bears repeating: what a relief.

I Can Hardly Wait

A second fruit of surrender is faith. And there is perhaps no better or more practical synonym for *faith* than *patience*.[16] Egyptian theologian Adel Bestavros writes, "Patience with others is Love, Patience with self is Hope, Patience with God is Faith."[17] Yet just as we moralize against passivity, waiting is seldom perceived as a positive experience. It's irritating at best and excruciating at worst—the

---

15. Kobe Campbell (@kobecampbell_), "Let the Worst Version of Yourself Be Loved," TikTok, June 24, 2022, https://www.tiktok.com/@kobecampbell_/video/7101324282357239086?refer=embed.

16. *Trust* comes close.

17. Adel Bestavros, quoted in Thomáš Halík, *Patience with God: The Story of Zacchaeus Continuing in Us* (Random House, 2009), v.

opposite of glamorous. Tell a friend you're taking your kids to Disney World, and if they've been there before, nine times out of ten they will give you advice about how to avoid the lines.[18] We do our best to minimize wait times wherever possible. And yet we spend so much of our lives doing exactly that: waiting.

When we're a kid, we wait to grow up. Once we're older, we wait to meet that special someone, then we wait for them to commit. We wait for a baby to arrive, and then once they're here, we wait for them to be out of diapers so that we can get a decent night's sleep. Once they're teenagers, we wait for their attitudes to improve, and after they're out of the house, we wait for them to call at the holidays. At work we wait for a promotion. Then perhaps we wait for retirement, or for our finances to be on strong enough ground to get there. In retirement, we wait for doctor's appointments, then for test results.

We wait for more global things as well. We wait for elections to pass, for wars to end, for justice to be done, for the day when "we'll walk as one and hardness of this life will be overcome."[19]

Sometimes it feels like waiting is all we ever do. Waiting does not come naturally to human beings, type A or type B, child or adult. We would much rather pounce than pause.

Waiting is a forced interruption to our control over our lives. When you are waiting, you've done everything you can to get a desired result—a table at a restaurant or admission to a college—and the ball is now in someone else's court. Those of us who struggle to relinquish control might pace while waiting in line or check the online portal every few hours (or seconds!) for a status update.

I know that for my own children, waiting is equivalent to discouragement. It is tantamount to not getting what they want. In the Bible, however, waiting is usually synonymous with believing. Isaiah claims that God "works for those who wait for him" (Isa.

18. The tenth time they'll tell you about saving money. Do not fall for the turkey legs!
19. The Killers, "Running Towards a Place," track 7 on *Imploding the Mirage*, UMG Recordings, 2020.

64:4). In the Sermon on the Mount, Jesus praises the birds of the air and the lilies of the field because of their complete reliance on—and surrender to—God's provision, which never fails (Matt. 6:26–30). God is the actor; they are the faithful. Later, Paul identifies patience as one of the fruits of the Spirit (Gal. 5:22). When we embrace the freedom to just wait, we are saying, "We believe in a God who will show up, who has things under control even when we don't."

Of course, it's a whole lot easier to wait when you know what's coming. That's when hope produces the perseverance that faithful passivity demands. When In-N-Out Burger opened their first franchise in Colorado, some customers waited in line for a mouthwatering fourteen hours to sample the legendary cheeseburger. I can only imagine how good those grease bombs tasted. The customers could endure the line because they were confident about what they'd receive at the end of it. That's what allowed them to surrender to the cars inching along in front of them.

And yet as delicious as these fruits (or burgers!) of surrender may be, the Big Relief does not lie in the injunction that you and I practice more honesty or cultivate more patience. The Big Relief has to do with the revelation that God is not waiting on you or me before he'll be our God. God doesn't wait to find out how devout or religious we are, or how humble and openhearted, before he showers us with love. He isn't waiting to find out if we're serious about him, or even if we believe in him. My favorite youth catechism frames the Big Relief this way:

> God has simply decided. God made this decision knowing full well the kind of person you are. God knows you better than anyone else could—inside out, upside down, and backwards. God knows where you are strong and where you are weak, what you are most proud of and what you would most like to hide. Be that as it may, God's decision is made. . . . This is the decision: God has decided to be *your* God. For God wants to be as close to you as your next breath, to be the one who gives you confidence and value, to open a future to you

in the freedom of the Word. God wants to be the one to whom you turn for whatever you need.[20]

The God of grace is not out to oppress you. The message of the gospel, in fact, is that God would rather surrender himself than allow his children to be swallowed by the paralyzing forces of sin and death. You could say he's a bit of a control freak that way.

20. James A. Nestingen and Gerhard O. Forde, *Free to Be: A Handbook to Luther's Small Catechism*, ed. Susan R. Niemi and Ann L. Rehfeldt (Augsburg Fortress, 1993), 5–6.

5

Atonement

The Relief from Guilt

"If you're anything like me, you spend about 87 percent of your mental life winning imaginary arguments that are never actually going to take place."[1] This confession from essayist Tim Kreider stopped me in my tracks when I read it. He was unmasking a truth I recognized, with some well-chosen hyperbole to drive the point home. The older I get, though, the less it feels like hyperbole. He may have been undershooting the percentage.

We construct these arguments all the time, usually as we're driving or taking a shower, and fragments often leak out into our everyday exchanges. Recently I listened as a friend laid out an elaborate and well-rehearsed case against his wife. His chief charge had to do with the light fixtures she'd recently purchased, which he felt were both superfluous and nonfunctional. He didn't understand why they had forked out more for brass bedside sconces than for their actual bed, especially since these things, he swore, shed less light than a candle. He then cited me the science on how much light the average middle-aged male needed to read, how his eyes weren't what they used to

1. Tim Kreider, *We Learn Nothing: Essays* (Simon & Schuster, 2012), 50.

be, and how now he was using his phone's flashlight in addition to the meager bulb. He was convinced that she resented how much he enjoyed science fiction before bed. After he showed me a picture of the setup, I remarked that it had a bit of a Charles Dickens charm. This was not the verdict he was looking for.

Later that day, my wife let me read a text chain with the moms of our son's baseball team. The coach had gotten a promotion at work and wasn't able to show up at practices as often, and a few of the parents weren't thrilled, especially not after the team's embarrassing loss that past Saturday. One mother, a former college athlete, shared the agenda she'd put together for her upcoming call with the coach. It had no fewer than twelve points, including one about pop-fly etiquette I'm pretty sure she'd borrowed verbatim from YouTube. "It's open and shut!" read the first blue bubble underneath.

"They've lost their minds," my wife said, sighing in sympathy for the underpaid twentysomething who was about to reap the whirl-wind. Doubtless the poor guy didn't realize he was on trial.

But I recognized the injured tone of the texts. I'd employed it myself earlier that day when, during a staff meeting, I let fly a piercing takedown of a critical email my organization had received that week. How dare a reader suggest that communication about our upcoming conference was lacking? Didn't they know how much we had on our plates? How short-staffed we were? Everyone sends too many emails anyway. If anyone is to blame, it's Google! Sheesh.

I'm reminded of the adage in Alcoholics Anonymous that the only thing better than being right is feeling wronged. Righteous indignation can be intoxicating. Another adage, not from AA, maintains that life is a journey. Maybe sometimes it is. Much of the time, however, life is a courtroom.

In the courtroom of life, we are tried in any number of ways, in matters great and small. We accuse and we defend. We cross-examine, collect evidence, recruit witnesses, and establish precedent.[2] We appeal

2. No one has done more to illustrate this aspect of life than comedian and writer Larry David, who chose to end both of his television masterworks—*Seinfeld* and *Curb*

and we object and we give speeches and, most of all, we judge. How many marriages devolve into plaintiffs and defendants, figuratively if not literally? How many parent-child relationships? Unfortunately, no matter where you sit in the courtroom of life, the conviction rate appears to be high and getting higher—if the guilt we feel is any indication.

Happy Mother's Day

The single most foot-in-mouth moment in my twenty years of public speaking happened on a Mother's Day. As anyone who has done time on a church staff knows, that's a banner Sunday. Lots of otherwise absent family members come out of the woodwork at their mom's behest. I'd been given the daunting task of preaching at four services that day.

I don't remember why I thought it would be wise to reference a recent cartoon by David Sipress in my sermon, but I am positive I didn't run it by my boss beforehand. A woman stands at a podium, giving the eulogy at her mother's funeral. The caption reads, "Mother wouldn't want us to feel sad—she'd want us to feel guilty."[3] You could've heard a pin drop. The discomfort was instantly visible in the congregation's body language, all eyes averted from the pulpit. It turns out that the subject of guilt is not funny, especially when it relates to your own parents, who may or may not be sitting beside you.

My point in mentioning the cartoon was not to prop up the tired stereotype of the guilt-mongering mother—moms suffer more than enough condemnation as it is. The point was that the criticisms that echo around our brains often assume the voice of someone who

---

Your Enthusiasm—in courtrooms. In each instance, the protagonists are found guilty on all charges, the main difference being that the latter series indicts the jurors as well.

3. David Sipress, "Mother Wouldn't Want Us to Feel Sad—She'd Want Us to Feel Guilty," *New Yorker*, August 10, 2016, https://condenaststore.com/featured/a-woman-dressed-in-black-speaks-at-her-mothers-david-sipress.html.

raised us. If you are a person who deals with guilt, you know of what I speak. There were three other services that day, and after my first sermon, my boss—who almost never vetoes content—*strongly* suggested I leave the cartoon on the cutting-room floor.

That was the day I learned that guilt is too powerful a force to speak about in a cavalier way. It is a painful and sometimes crippling reality for a great many of us, even in a culture that has repudiated what it considers to be the source of that guilt: 1950s social norms, the church, perfectionism, and so on. Guilt's "strange persistence" represents one of the biggest quandaries at the heart of modern life.[4] If the world is becoming less religious and codes of morality more diffuse, why do we still feel so condemned? This persistence is strange because guilt is, by definition, tied to transgression. You did wrong according to some standard of morality and are therefore saddled with culpability. Yet if we cannot agree on right and wrong—if such a distinction even exists in any meaningful way—then wouldn't guilt be *less* pronounced today rather than more?

My main theory, which I outline in *Seculosity*, has to do with what philosopher Charles Taylor calls the Nova Effect.[5] As trust in a shared moral authority has eroded, the result has not been an absence of such authority but a multiplication of it. A rush of strident voices has filled the void left by capital-*R* Religion, with more voices popping up every day. This means that instead of (or in addition to) God's wagging finger, we contend with the wagging finger of Madison Avenue, the weight scale, the social media algorithm, the legal system, the parenting industrial complex, our children's history books, our neighbors on Nextdoor, and so on.[6] Everywhere we turn,

---

4. Wilfred M. McClay, "The Strange Persistence of Guilt: And Its Infinite Extensibility," *Hedgehog Review* 19, no. 1 (Spring 2017), https://hedgehogreview.com/issues/the-post-modern-self/articles/the-strange-persistence-of-guilt.

5. See Charles Taylor, *A Secular Age* (Belknap, 2007), 299.

6. For those mercifully unaware of Nextdoor, it's an app that's meant to function as a virtual bulletin board for neighborhoods—anybody seen our cat?—but frequently devolves into a venue for mutual surveillance, finger-pointing, and outright bigotry. Yuck.

someone or something stands ready to condemn us. Prosecutors abound. Some even greet us when we look in the mirror.[7]

As a result, our sense of guilt is simultaneously crushing and free-floating. Different people feel guilty for different things. Maybe we feel survivor's guilt, maybe White guilt, maybe Catholic guilt, maybe liberal guilt, maybe mom guilt, maybe climate guilt, maybe all of the above. Maybe we feel guilty about something we did, maybe about something we failed to do. Maybe we feel guilty for something our ancestors or national leaders did. Maybe we feel *too* guilty about certain things and not enough about others. Maybe we feel guilty about not feeling guilty enough. The snake can eat its tail pretty quickly on this one.

We may not be able to pin down precisely why we feel guilty today; we just know we do. We don't always know what law we've transgressed; we just know we have.

Slanted and Enchanted

When I was growing up, one of the primary refrains in the cultural discourse had to do with absolute truth. Young people at the schools I attended had begun to embrace a more situational or "postmodern" understanding of right and wrong: "What's true for you may not be true for me," and so forth. Traditionally minded people, in contrast, upheld the virtues of Truth—with a capital *T*—that apply to all people. They believed, especially if they were religious, that morality is God-given and therefore transcends context. All throughout my adolescence, cultural conservatives rang the alarm bell about the threat of moral relativism and the chaos that would run wild in a loosey-goosey secular world that had lost its bearings.

Their children—and at the time it felt a lot more like old versus young than right versus left—welcomed the shades of gray. Cultivating a little detachment from moral absolutes would not only guard

7. Indeed, anytime you hear someone fess to being their own worst critic, they are saying, to some degree, that they are their own prosecuting attorney.

against destructive forms of shame but also allow people to get along in an increasingly pluralistic society. This detachment sometimes translated into a culture of apathy. In practice this meant that my generation, known today as Generation X, considered caring about anything too much to be profoundly uncool. Irony, not sincerity, was our currency, as we listened to Pavement and watched *Seinfeld*. About the worst spiritual crime you could commit was selling out— that is, caring about something as phony as bourgeois success. Guilt was for people who took things too seriously, a relic from an earlier uptight age.

These brushstrokes are broad, so I hope you'll forgive any imprecision. I hope you'll also forgive me for not expounding on what happened to this stream of thought.[8] It's enough to say that whatever moral relativism Generation X snuck into the Zeitgeist, it did not stick around. Today, moral certainty reigns supreme, and not just among older or religious people. It's bewildering for a lot of us who attended high school in the 1990s. Our certainties today differ according to ideological location—and often conflict violently with one another—but no one would accuse our present moment of moral laxity. The seriousness is off the charts, and so is the guilt, not to mention the self-righteousness. Just spend five minutes on X (formerly Twitter). Pharisees are running the show: morning, noon, and night.

In her book *What If This Were Enough?*, Heather Havrilesky reflects on her years of giving public advice to young people through her Ask Polly column. She notes that many of the common assumptions about millennials—for example, that they are entitled and overconfident—have proven untrue. She writes, "What I discover in my email inbox each morning are dispatches from young people who feel guilty and inadequate at every turn and who compare themselves relentlessly to others."[9] Havrilesky then offers a representative submission from a reader: "I think my primary emotion is guilt. . . .

8. Chuck Klosterman's book *The Nineties: A Book* (Penguin, 2022) sheds some light.
9. Heather Havrilesky, *What If This Were Enough?* (Penguin Random House, 2018), 115.

When I am happy, it only takes moments before I feel guilty about it—I feel desperately unworthy of my happiness, guilty for receiving it out of the pure chaotic luck of the universe."[10]

You'll notice that the writer does not refer to what they feel guilty about. Guilt is more a default state of being, exerting constant pressure and wreaking havoc on mental health. In left-of-center circles, many people feel pressure to demonstrate their contrition and regret over cycles of injustice. The expressions thereof can get competitive. In right-of-center circles, many people feel pressure to assert their innocence and reject any framework that might imply otherwise. Either way, we all feel judged, pretty much all the time. This makes sense, since we're all judging one another (and ourselves) pretty much all the time.

I do not mean to suggest that guilt is always bad. It may be a negative emotion, but in proper measure, guilt serves a positive and necessary function. When one of my boys lies to me or says something mean to their brothers, I want them to feel badly about it. I'd be concerned if they didn't. Their remorse reflects a capacity for empathy and love. It is an essential ingredient to them learning to behave better. Sociopaths don't feel guilt, which is a big part of what allows them to dehumanize others and commit reprehensible crimes.

Guilt can be useful spiritually too. It leads to repentance, which leads, God willing, to absolution. Without guilt, a word like *forgiveness* would have no substance. There would be nothing to forgive, no reason to ever say sorry. The psychic pressure of guilt—its sting, to paraphrase Saint Paul—can be a benefit insofar as it leads us to look for relief, which, in the best of cases, means God.

Guilt Management 101

The nature of guilt is that it's burdensome. That burden is heavy and begs to be unloaded. A mentor of mine once characterized guilt

10. Havrilesky, *What If This Were Enough?*, 116.

as having a mind of its own, always prowling the surroundings in search of a place to discharge. The guilt-ridden person scans the horizon for someone or something that might shoulder the burden for them. Not all the solutions they find are successful or advisable.

Escape, for example, is a common strategy for coping with guilt. Addicts talk about the respite that substances give them from internal accusation. They speak of drugs that silence the relentless regrets that plague their consciences. If only the self-recrimination didn't return the next day with such a vengeance, having added another binge to the mounting pile of accusatory evidence. There are plenty of escape hatches that don't involve narcotics, though. I've spoken to runners who crave exercise because it allows them to "turn off their brains for a while." They're not talking about a break from imaginative problem-solving; they are talking about a recess from the courtroom within. Of course, physical activity doesn't always have this effect. A dear friend of mine lives in a beautiful part of the country. She longs for rainy days because on those days she doesn't have to feel guilty for not being outdoors. She can rest.

Another popular method of off-loading guilt is the one social media affords us with such immediacy: deflection. We condemn other people from behind the safety of our screens as a way of preventing anyone from looking too closely at the skeletons in our closet. Pointing out a stranger's wrongdoing has the added advantage of aligning us with the innocent. If we are holding bad actors to account, we must be on the side of the angels, right? Nothing to see here; move along. Philosopher Mark Edmundson claims that the entire internet evolved to serve this purpose, which he equates with Sigmund Freud's conception of the superego.[11] Of course, those judgments have a way of boomeranging on us at inconvenient times.

Then there's what may be the most tempting and prevalent method of dealing with guilt: denial. Perhaps you know someone who's never, ever wrong about anything. People like this are a tough breed to

11. Mark Edmundson, *The Age of Guilt: The Super-Ego in the Online World* (Yale University Press, 2023).

love. Or perhaps you've heard someone insist that "there is no such thing as a guilty pleasure." (Tell that to one of the addicts above.) Or maybe, when trying to feel okay about flaking on a commitment to others, you've told yourself that "guilt is just a social construct. You're actually being brave by rejecting it!" We believe that if we say these things often enough, eventually we'll believe them. But guilt doesn't work that way. I remember trying to comfort a friend going through a divorce by telling him he had nothing to feel guilty about—his ex had given him no choice. He balked at the statement, saying that even though it hadn't been primarily his fault or decision, he'd always feel guilty that the marriage fell apart. It was impossible not to when he looked at his children; choice had nothing to do with it. He was right. Desperation itself never absolved anyone of anything. Indeed, the louder our assertions of innocence, the less convincing they become.

This does not mean that all guilt is created equal. Much of the guilt we feel *is* trumped-up, illegitimate, or manufactured. A woman I know felt terribly guilty for gaining weight after her second baby was born, despite her loved ones' assurance that it was perfectly natural and healthy. Nothing saddens me more than when my middle son apologizes for asking for help with his math homework because he feels guilty for pulling me away from what I'm doing. That sort of guilt should be contested whenever it arises.

Unfortunately, whether we should or shouldn't feel guilty about something rarely has much bearing on if we do. Guilt seldom yields to reason.

Atonement Happens

What guilt does yield to, however, is atonement. *Atonement* is a fancy word for making amends. It refers to any action we undertake to make up for wrongdoing. It includes the cost we pay to repair alienation, the effort we expend to secure reconciliation between estranged parties. Reparations are a form of atonement, for instance, and so is incarceration. You'll note that neither of these is pleasant, and both involve suffering. This is why, of all the aforementioned guilt management strategies, we usually turn to atonement last.

Atonement may be a religious-sounding word, yet it takes many nonreligious forms. Some of these forms are constructive, and some are not. Self-flagellation, in which we consciously punish ourselves by inflicting pain on our bodies, tends to be an unhealthy form. This ranges from small acts of self-negation like fasting to more serious ones like cutting. Maybe you've met someone who refuses to leave an abusive relationship because they feel, on some level, it is the only way they can make right the mistake they made in getting into that relationship. Leaving would only compound the guilt.

On the healthier end, activism can be a form of atonement. Scions of wealthy families dedicate their lives to atoning for the sins of their profiteering ancestors via philanthropy and advocacy. A man who served at our church went into ministry in his early sixties partly to atone for the moral compromises he'd made in his career as a corporate lawyer. I know a woman who felt so guilty about the damage she believed she'd done through her work as a fashion model that she devoted the rest of her life to working with nonprofits providing body-positive resources for girls.

Unfortunately, this kind of perpetual atonement can become enslaving if it offers no completion, or what theologians would call satisfaction. Regret can turn a person in on themselves in a never-ending quest to do enough good to erase the guilt. But experience teaches that the finish line does not exist. There is always one more good deed to do, one more apology to give before the slate is wiped clean. Partial atonement wears us out.

Some versions of Christianity invite people into religious forms of partial atonement that mimic these nonreligious forms. To be "made right" with God you must pray these prayers, read these verses, give away this amount of money, serve this number of underprivileged people, advocate this loudly for these causes. And you must never cease doing so. Such invitations may mean well—these are all good things, after all—but they miss what makes the Christian vision of atonement such a Big Relief. They miss the once-and-for-all finality of Calvary.

Atonement lies at the heart of what Christians believe occurred in the crucifixion of Jesus Christ. When the apostle John writes that Christ's death constitutes an "atoning sacrifice for our sins, and not for ours only but also for the sins of the whole world," he means that, on the cross, Jesus assumed the full guilt incurred by sin— guilt that is rightfully ours (1 John 2:2). Jesus suffered its terminal consequence and then rose to new life, reconciling sinful men and women to a holy God. On Good Friday, the burden of human guilt found its willing off-ramp. The blameless Christ not only took on sin but *became* sin so that "in him we might become the righteousness of God" (2 Cor. 5:21). This is often called the "glorious exchange."

In her magisterial work *The Crucifixion*, Fleming Rutledge writes, "The plain sense of the New Testament taken as a whole gives the strong impression that Jesus gave himself up to shame, spitting, scourging, and a degrading public death before the eyes of the whole world, not only for our sake but also in our place."[12]

Unlike our halting attempts to make up for the wrongs we've done, the atonement Christ has made is total and final. *The Book of Common Prayer*, which governs my tradition, describes his death as "a full, perfect, and sufficient sacrifice, oblation, and satisfaction, for the sins of the whole world."[13] There is nothing left.

The grace of this atonement lies in its vicariousness—meaning, atonement has been made *for* you but not *by* you. This is why Christians talk fondly and frequently of substitution. In the final trial of life's courtroom, Jesus takes our seat and accepts the verdict due us. He substitutes himself for you and me—not only absorbing our condemnation but also lending us his own righteousness. As a

---

12. Fleming Rutledge, *The Crucifixion: Understanding the Death of Jesus Christ* (Eerdmans, 2015), 529.

13. *The Book of Common Prayer and Administration of the Sacraments and Other Rites and Ceremonies of the Church: Together with the Psalter or Psalms of David According to the Use of the Episcopal Church* (Seabury Press, 1979), 334.

result, you and I are set free. When folk musicians sing about being washed in the blood of the lamb, this is what they are getting at: an inversion of judicial prudence so profound that when it's grasped, its subjects are doused in astonishment and gratitude of the most generative kind.

And yet profound as this aspect may be, the cross does not reduce entirely to guilt and atonement. It is an event that runs thick with meaning, no strand of which necessarily cancels out the others. In submitting to crucifixion, for instance, Jesus refuses to repay the condemnation he suffers at the hands of the crowds and authorities with condemnation of his own. Instead, he turns the other cheek and demonstrates the radical extent of God's love. Jesus would rather die than strike back in violence. Furthermore, in dying and rising again, Jesus defeats sin and death, once and for all, breaking the chains of iniquity that bind us. Theologians refer to Jesus in this regard as *Christus Victor*, and one could spend a lifetime pondering the glory of that victory.

These various elements (and others!) coexist and are not in competition with one another, however much Christians may sometimes treat them that way. At different times in our lives, different aspects of the cross will have greater or lesser purchase on our hearts, and that's okay. To those who have been victimized by injustice and evil, the announcement of Christ's triumph over the powers of darkness will resonate on a special frequency. To those weighed down by guilt, the atonement that Jesus makes on behalf of sinners will speak with particular immediacy and depth.

Over My Dead Body

Many people, it must be said, protest this reading of the crucifixion. Very few words in the theological lexicon provoke as much controversy or disdain among Christians as the word *substitution*. For those who grew up in more conservative church settings, it conjures up images of a punitive, bloodthirsty tyrant in the sky who exacts his pound of flesh by torturing and killing his only child (and inspiring others to do the same). They view such a notion as simplistic and gruesome—a far cry from the good shepherd we meet in Jesus. I've run into many clergy who balk at what they call "atonement theology" and aim to remove any such language from their church services. This is not an easy task if you read any liturgies written before 1980 or so. Still, one can't help sympathizing with the attempt to avoid painting pictures of God that could be interpreted as mean, capricious, or abusive.

To be clear, the doctrine of substitutionary atonement—what Rutledge calls "the motif of substitution"—has proved no less immune to weaponizing than any other Christian doctrine. Misgivings about its brutality are voiced by real people carrying real baggage who, in many cases, are seeking to safeguard others from experiencing similar trauma. The urge to cement kindness at the center of God's character should never be faulted. I merely want to register three observations from decades of fielding such objections, lest we diminish the potential relief on offer.

A favorite writer of mine, psychologist and theologian Richard Beck, used to share the revulsion described above. Then he started running a Bible study with inmates at a maximum-security prison. He discovered that few spiritual concerns were more pressing among the inmates than guilt and forgiveness. The felons he met forced him to reevaluate his aversion to preaching atonement:

> Here's the thing, guilt is a problem. Shame is a curse. They really are. Consequently, forgiveness and grace are needed. Visions of atonement that address shame and guilt are dealing with deep and vital human concerns. . . .
>
> Should you, for example, use forensic metaphors with children and young people, cranking up the guilt to get a big emotional response from them at the end of your rally, retreat or camp experience? Probably not. But you might lean into forensic metaphors when working with people who have committed crimes that haunt them, who wonder if they can ever be forgiven for the horrible things they have done. Yeah, you might talk with these people about how their

sins have been forgiven and their guilt washed away by the blood of the Lamb.[14]

In other words, it is a lot easier to eschew "atonement theology" when you haven't been convicted of any crimes—or when life circumstances have allowed you to avoid guilty exposure thus far. And so, my first observation is that sometimes the aversion to atonement theology is, in fact, an aversion to the concept of guilt itself, afforded by privilege and fortified by prosperity. Heaven forbid we find ourselves in the hot seat one day because the doctrine may take on a more attractive light. That's an admittedly somber thing to say, and Lord knows I do not wish anyone such an ordeal. But the incarcerated may have access to truths about the human condition that are unavailable to those of us who have skated by.

Second, an across-the-board objection to substitution often betrays an eccentric and imprecise understanding of the Trinity. Descriptions of substitutionary atonement as "cosmic child abuse" imply that the Son is fully distinct from and subordinate to the Father, subject to the Father's authority and action.[15] But God is three in one. He does not oppose himself. If Jesus stands in our place, it is God himself doing so. You might say that Jesus does not die on the cross *in order* for God to love us but *because* God loves us. This means that certain harsh and punitive ways of teaching atonement theology—for example, any implication that God *wants* to punish us until Jesus steps in—miss the trinitarian nature of the cross just as much as the divine child-abuse caricature.

Third, substitution possesses uncanny emotional gravity. Whenever a film or book ends with an act of self-sacrifice, we weep at the beauty of it, not the horror. Watch *Mare of Easttown* if you don't believe me. Or *The Holdovers*. Or *The Lives of Others*. Read *A Tale*

14. Richard Beck, "Reading the Bible with the Damned: Part 3, Guilt and Forgiveness," *Experimental Theology*, Substack, February 19, 2023, https://richardbeck.substack.com/p/reading-the-bible-with-the-damned-980.
15. This is called Arianism and was condemned as a heresy at the Council of Nicaea in AD 325.

of Two Cities. Or *Harry Potter*. Or *True Grit*. When one person dies so that another may live, or when one person suffers so another may flourish, the reflexive response of the human heart is tectonic. Such outpourings are not arbitrary, socialized, or somehow "wrong." They reveal something important about the nature of love—namely, that love is perfected in pain, not apart from it. "Love hurts" is what the song says, much as I wish it weren't true. When the apostle John talks about Jesus's atoning sacrifice, it is in the context of expounding on God's love (1 John 4:10). The love of God, he reminds us, is not a marshmallow cloud of rom-com clichés. Love that has power is the kind that suffers, the kind that bleeds. Love places the other's comfort over one's own.

Legendary Italian free diver Alessia Zecchini witnessed this earth-shattering truth firsthand. Free diving is sometimes called the world's most dangerous sport. In free diving, athletes compete to reach the lowest ocean depth without an air tank. Since brain damage from oxygen deprivation is not uncommon, each diver must be accompanied by a safety diver. When Zecchini set the world record in 2017 (104 meters, or 341 feet!), she did so with the help of safety diver and trainer Stephen Keenan. After the goal was reached—and the two had fallen in love—Keenan invited Zecchini to come train at his dive center in Dahab, Egypt, site of the infamous arch of the Blue Hole. It is infamous because the route has killed more divers than any other on the planet. To make it through the arch, you must dive down fifty meters and then traverse an underwater tunnel thirty meters long before making your ascent on the other side. If you mistime the attempt even slightly, the tunnel will trap you. Only one female had ever accomplished this feat, and Zecchini was determined to become the second.

When the day of her historic attempt finally arrived, something went wrong. Zecchini lost sight of the rope that would take her back to the surface on the other side of the tunnel. When you're that far under water, with that little oxygen, disorientation is a major problem. Despite missing their rendezvous point—with precious seconds ticking by—Keenan finally reached Zecchini and started guiding his champion girlfriend back to the surface. As they got close, however, he realized that both of them were going to black out, her first. Survival depended on them emerging from the depths on their backs so that they'd be able to get air while unconscious. Cameras that had been put in place to capture the attempt show Keenan using his last moments of lucidity to position Zecchini this way. In order to do so, however, he had to remain on his front, face down. Only one of them could survive the ordeal. Keenan ensured it was Zecchini. He died so that she might live.[16] "The good shepherd lays down his life for the sheep" is how Jesus describes what happened (John 10:11).

Say Amen, Somebody

One of the greatest arguments for the existence of God was made in 1982. That it didn't receive anywhere near a Thomas Aquinas–level of attention is a great sadness to me and something I pray we'll see rectified in years to come. I'm referring to the documentary *Say Amen, Somebody*. Directed by George Nierenberg, the film was the first feature-length attempt to document the history and artistry of Black gospel music. The documentary predates much of the genre's commercialization and captures the form at its most authentic and sublime. I would invite anyone tempted to dismiss the Christian faith to invest a hundred minutes in watching it.

Thomas Dorsey, the "Father of Gospel Music," appears on camera throughout, but the real star is singer Willie Mae Ford Smith, or Mama Smith, who was seventy-seven at the time of filming. Joy, talent, and what can only be called holiness drip from her every pore. We watch as she blesses everyone she encounters, regardless of race or creed, smiling and laughing and giving contagious praise

---

16. Their story is documented in *The Deepest Breath*, directed by Laura McGann (A24; Motive Films; Ventureland; RAW TV, 2023), Netflix, https://www.netflix.com/title/81630917. Zecchini now lives in the shadow of that love, which sustains and inspires her. Each and every time she sets a new record, she dedicates the feat to Keenan.

to God. Yet as soul stirring as Smith's presence is, she is nearly upstaged about two-thirds of the way through the film by a set of dapper twins, Eddie and Edgar O'Neal. At a tribute concert for Mama Smith, the O'Neal Twins bring the house down with a song called "Jesus Dropped the Charges." The song conveys the Big Relief in purely judicial terms yet without one iota of the dry proceduralism that forensic understandings of guilt and atonement sometimes portend.

The lyrics, which were written by Pastor Richard White, begin with the admission, "I was guilty of all charges, doomed and disgraced."[17] It's worth noting that the performance takes place in Antioch Baptist Church in inner-city St. Louis, with a crowd full of locals who were likely (and sadly) overacquainted with accusations of criminality. "But Jesus, with his special love, saved me by his grace," the twins jubilantly intone, just before bellowing the title phrase in the chorus. As they paraphrase the words of the prophet Zephaniah—"The LORD has taken away the judgments against you" (3:15)—the joy in the room turns feverish, and scores of immaculately dressed attendees dance in the aisles.

Later in the song, we hear how Jesus lifted "my heavy load," and then, as if to make the connection to Christ's own suffering explicit, Edgar and Eddie reach the bridge: "At Calvary I heard him say, 'Case dismissed!'" At this point the excitement is ricocheting off the walls, and the church completes its transformation from courthouse to dance hall. Eddie vamps the key line from the Gospel of John: "It is finished" (19:30).

Descriptions of ecstasy can only ever be poor approximations of the real thing, I realize. But the source of elation in the performance is more than just musical. These men are preaching the relief of grace, and indeed, that's their mission as they articulate it elsewhere. To those bowed down by guilt, the O'Neal Twins proclaim full acquittal and final exoneration. The burden has, in an ultimate sense, been

---

17. The O'Neal Twins, "Jesus Dropped the Charges," track 4 on *Saved by His Love*, Savoy Records, 1981.

taken off our shoulders, yours and mine. There is nothing left for us to carry. What a relief!

Dolly Parton once said that "grief is love with no place to go."[18] If that's true, then despair is guilt with no place to go. The Christian faith gives guilt a destination. The foot of the cross is our guilt depository. You can leave your burden there, confident that full atonement has been made. Court is adjourned—for good.

18. *Christmas on the Square*, directed by Debbie Allen (Warner Bros. Television, 2020), Netflix, https://www.netflix.com/title/81128934.

6

Imputation

The Relief from Status Anxiety

Here is an incomplete list of things I've seen used—or used my-self—to signify status in the past month or so: dollars, zip codes, party invitations, advanced degrees, body mass index, golf handi-caps, busyness, hair color (and length), engine horsepower, house cleanliness, soccer trophies, knowledge of current events, number of bedrooms, number of tattoos, number of children, number of page views, biceps size, audience size, waist size, mental health di-agnosis, pronoun usage, literary tastes, children's school, church denomination, charitable giving, mileage run per week, passport stamps, carbon footprint, and graveyard plot location.

Another status symbol might be the ability to see through status symbols the quickest—or feign the most indifference to them. We are extraordinarily imaginative creatures when it comes to symbol-izing and signaling status.

It could be that I live in a particularly status-conscious place dur-ing a particularly status-conscious time. I suspect, however, that human beings have always been caught up in status games of one kind or another. Digital technology has simply made it easier to play them. We have far more opportunity to establish, compare, and bicker over social rankings than we once did. The venues where we do so are open and active twenty-four hours a day.

But status seeking predates smartphones (and will outlast them too). It is not a uniquely modern or Western phenomenon, at least not if the seminar on the Indian caste system I took in college is any indication. The yearning for a measure of our value, which is all status really is, seems to be something universal—and instinctually human.[1] All of us, no matter where or when we live, need to feel like we have value. We need to know that we are worthy not just of consideration but respect, that our lives have weight and meaning— that we matter!

In 1948 the anthropologist William Bascom reported on a status convention on the Micronesian island of Pohnpei. Apparently, each year the men of the island compete to see who can grow the largest yam. At the end of the year, the chief announces a winner, and a special feast is held in the winner's honor. The status on offer inspires the men to raise their yams in far-off plots, which often takes years of secret labor to do well. It is not unheard of for them to creep out of bed in the middle of the night to go water their crop.[2]

As silly and convoluted as status games often become, the human hunger for validation is not silly or convoluted. To live without any status whatsoever is to live without dignity.

Some cultures are up front about status, such as those in East Africa, where disclosure of parentage and prestige precedes most interactions. Life in the military may be difficult in many ways, but I'm told the open acknowledgment of rank can be refreshing, as it frees a person from less direct forms of jockeying.

Those of us in the United States currently live in a deeply status-conscious culture that avoids openly discussing the subject. There's

---

1. *Human* may be too confining a category, as the animal kingdom plays its own status games. The term *alpha male* was coined in relation to primates, not CEOs.

2. Will Storr, *The Status Game: On Social Position and How We Use It* (HarperCollins, 2021), 28–29.

something taboo about "going there" in most situations, something uncomfortable about surfacing this stuff in public. Instead, we allow it to lurk under the surface of conversation. We ask a person where they went to school or where they went on vacation, and the subtext is "Are you above or below me?" The more insecure we're feeling, the more transparent these volleys become.

As the venues for establishing status have widened, the symbols have multiplied, and so too have the associated pressures. Consider the pressure to excel, which derives in large part from the status we confer on those who achieve difficult things. If you've ever yearned to get your name in the paper—or the history books—you know what I'm talking about. Our education system relies on this form of status seeking to function, just as much if not more than it does on knowledge seeking. That is, the esteem associated with acceptance to an Ivy League school is not incidental, certainly not when it comes to sweatshirt sales. The logo reflects the value not only of someone's transcript but also of their very self.

A Crisis of Mattering

In her book *Never Enough*, Jennifer Breheny Wallace details the plight of a group of unexpectedly at-risk children. Traditionally the groups considered most at risk in the United States have been children in foster care and children with incarcerated parents. Girls and boys in those circumstances have an increased likelihood of suffering from depression, substance abuse, and self-harm. In 2020, Wallace came across reports that included another group in this unfortunate cluster: the predominantly upper-middle-class children who attend "high-achieving schools." Prep school kids from affluent homes had somehow become the third most at-risk group for these debilitating afflictions.[3]

The conventional wisdom is that a large share of the blame falls on social media and the "toxic benchmarking" experienced there. But

3. Jennifer Breheny Wallace, *Never Enough: When Achievement Culture Becomes Toxic—and What We Can Do about It* (Penguin Random House, 2023), xiv–xvi.

Wallace identifies a deeper problem. In an interview with Professor Scott Galloway, she says,

> Social media is certainly a magnifier and an accelerant to these toxic pressures but it's not the root of it. The root of this is a lack of mattering universally. A lack of feeling valued for who we are at our core. We feel valued now for what we achieve, how much money we make. Society tells us certain people matter more. "Those influencers matter more." "Those with the most likes matter more." What I see as a social media crisis is a crisis of *mattering* and that goes much deeper than social media.

The real problem for this group, Wallace claims, is not primarily behavioral but internal. I would go so far as to call it spiritual. "A crisis of mattering" fuels the dysfunctional use of tech, not the other way around. She goes on to cite research that says, "The kids who were struggling the most felt like their mattering was contingent on their performance; that their parents only valued or cared about them when they were performing: 'I only matter to the extent I'm excelling according to this absurdly narrow set of metrics.'"[4]

According to her theory, children and parents alike have lost—or have had taken from them—a sense of mattering inherent to being alive. How this happened is debatable. It could have to do with the breakdown of trust in public institutions or the increasing atomization of American life described earlier. It might be related to the retreat from shared faith in God. Whatever the case, in response to this vacuum, we have outsourced our dignity to Silicon Valley and our nation's college admissions departments—a mandate far beyond (and even alien to) the purposes for which either was established.

It's easy to throw up one's hands at parents who have placed their children on the treadmills of travel sports and summer internships

---

4. Scott Galloway, "Conversation with Jennifer B. Wallace—What to Do About Toxic Achievement Culture," *The Prof G Pod with Scott Galloway* podcast, August 24, 2023, https://podcasts.apple.com/us/podcast/conversation-with-jennifer-b-wallace-what-to-do -about/id1498802610?i=1000625523187.

and standardized test prep. It's easy to judge them. Allow me to voice two caveats, though, as this is the milieu in which I am raising three boys. First, when I speak to my peers about the insanity of achievement culture, by and large they acknowledge the absurdity. They usually regret taking part but feel powerless to resist it. The cost of avoidance seems just too high, and none of us want our children to pay that cost. We parents love our kids and are genuinely afraid about what the future holds. And so we do everything in our power to set our kids up for future security, even when economic and cultural conditions seem to make that task more difficult with each passing year.[5]

Second, you don't avoid the pressure to matter by avoiding the pursuit of "excellence." Those who reject conventional status markers—the best schools, biggest houses, largest salaries, and so on—still want to be special; they're just interested in a different form of specialness.

One way the pressure to matter expresses itself in nonachievement terms today falls under the label of "identity." When people decry the logjam of "identity politics," they are usually decrying the highly contested ways we confer status to people according to an identity marker of some kind. The marker in question could be something low stakes, like the clothes we wear or the music we listen to. More often it is something closely held, like our ethnicity or our gender. It is not uncommon today to link our specialness to something we've suffered, like an injustice or an illness. It can be anything, really.[6] The moment we lean on a personal characteristic for specialness is the moment we make it vulnerable to status concerns—in competition

5. During the promotional cycle for *Never Enough*, I read some commentary that was trying to be kind to the parents in these enclaves. Someone somewhere trotted out data saying that it is, in fact, far harder to outearn one's parents now than ever before and that a great deal of the anxiety is economic, not existential. In other words, the reason we push kids into majors for super lucrative careers and away from the humanities is not just that we're more superficial but that economic factors have squeezed things so much that there's no security outside of banking jobs. We'll explore the underlying acceleration in the next chapter.

6. Except for social class. For contemporary Americans, class remains the most uncomfortable (yet extraordinarily significant) aspect of personal identity, a specter which lurks, unacknowledged, behind many other markers.

with the specialness of those around us. Such competition tends not to bring out the best in anyone. But the fierceness with which we assert our specialness—whatever it may be—reflects the pressure to matter that we're all living under.

Thou Shalt Have a Thing

What we're talking about here is really the pressure to be some-body, to be somebody of note, somebody worth taking seriously—somebody and not nobody. Indeed, underneath much of our bluster about status lies a fear about not being enough. Some commentators have termed this "status anxiety." We believe, on some level, that we are not enough as we are and require some distinguishing credential to give us value or bring us affection. Thus we spend our days franti-cally trying to demonstrate that we're worthy of the resources we consume and the space we occupy. *Self-justification* is the theological term that describes this pursuit.

Again, no one escapes the pressure to be somebody entirely. At some point in your life, probably when you were young, you felt it intensely. Back in 2007, in response to a Pew survey, 81 percent of eighteen-to-twenty-five-year-olds indicated that being rich was their number one or number two life goal, with 51 percent saying the same thing for being famous.[7] One can only imagine what those numbers would be like now in the "Age of the Influencer." This reflects a culture that worships at the altar of exceptionalism. I remember asking the kids at our church, during a children's sermon, what they wanted to be when they grew up and feeling dismayed when one of them blurted out, "YouTuber!" Dismayed but not surprised. It was my kid, after all.

But there are less overt ways that the process of self-definition becomes a burden. When kids are little, it is very common for parents

7. The Pew Research Center, "How Young People View Their Lives, Futures and Politics: A Portrait of 'Generation Next,'" January 9, 2007, 12, https://www.pewresearch.org/wp-content/uploads/sites/4/legacy-pdf/300.pdf.

to talk about them "finding their thing."[8] As in, we parents put them in a bunch of different activities in the hopes that they will find something they enjoy and, more important, are good at. "My kid just hasn't found his thing yet," I've heard many a parent confess in relation to a floundering preteen. I've said it myself. We are hoping our child finds an activity they can get excited about, where they can grow and develop confidence. What the pressure to "find our thing" often turns into, however, is a search for a workable identity—a ladder to get on as early as possible for the sake of future success and status. What would it mean if our kid never found their thing? Nothing good.

Thankfully, this pressure tends to abate as we grow older. Loss has a way of diminishing status as a motivator in human affairs. A parent dies, and we find we no longer care as much about career success. Or we recover from a serious illness and realize that we've spent far too much mental energy on how many people like our social media content. Suffering can be a potent means of relief from the pressure to justify ourselves. But detachment is one thing; grace is quite another.

Nobody's Somebody or Somebody's Nobody?

While our responses to the pressure to be somebody are as varied as we are, approaches commonly fall into two categories. Psychologist Joanna Collicutt McGrath classifies these as the "internal" style of attribution and—you guessed it—the "external" style.[9] The terms may sound a bit jargony, but the distinction they refer to is a simple and very useful one.

An internal style of attribution looks within for an answer to the question of our somebodyness. We ask ourselves, What is it about

---

8. With gratitude to Jordan Griesbeck's piece, "Thou Shalt Have a Thing," Mockingbird, December 14, 2023, https://mbird.com/social-science/parenting/thou-shalt-have-a-thing/.

9. Joanna Collicutt McGrath and Alister McGrath, *Self-Esteem: The Cross and Christian Confidence* (Crossway, 2002).

me that makes me worthy of attention? What traits of mine make me lovable? Say we believe our physical beauty gives us value. Without it, it's not that we don't know who we are, but we wonder if we're anything at all. And so we fight aging tooth and nail. It's not the smoothness of our skin that's in danger but our lovability. Or maybe we believe, unconsciously or not, that we can tell how important a person is by their real estate portfolio. Before long we're spending money we don't have to purchase property we don't need. In both cases, we presume that our status is linked to something we possess. The internal style of attribution is really the default style.

If only it worked. Anne Lamott once gave a graduation speech in which she talked about what happened after she started to experience success with her writing. She recalls getting published and slowly garnering the literary respect she'd aspired to as a student: "I got a lot of things that society had promised would make me whole and fulfilled—all the things that the culture tells you from preschool on will quiet the throbbing anxiety inside you—stature, the respect of colleagues, maybe even a kind of low-grade fame. The culture says these things will save you, as long as you also manage to keep your weight down. But the culture lies."[10]

Hanging our self-worth on the hook of internal attribution puts enormous pressure on us to establish, cultivate, and assert our some-bodyness. Yet the deeper problem is that the peace we believe we'll find at the top of the ladder of self-justification isn't there. Status games, we discover, are shell games, incapable of delivering the enoughness they promise.

I think of professional tennis player Naomi Osaka, who won the US Open in 2018 and 2020, setting the record for the most money earned in a single year by any female athlete ever. At the height of her success, Osaka experienced firsthand the bait and switch that Lamott describes. In 2021, she dropped out of the French Open for mental health reasons and then refused to play at Wimbledon, where

10. Anne Lamott, "Let Us Commence," *Salon*, June 6, 2003, https://www.salon.com/2003/06/06/commencement/.

she would have been one of the top seeds. That fall, she entered the 2021 US Open, where she was defending champion, but after losing in the third round, Osaka held a press conference where she exhibited rare candor for an elite athlete: "I feel like for me recently, when I win I don't feel happy. I feel more like a relief. And then when I lose, I feel very sad. I don't think that's normal. [*crying*] I honestly don't know when I'm going to play my next tennis match."[11]

Internal attribution failed Osaka. Instead of manifesting happiness or contentment, her success on the ladder of achievement produced anxiety, despair, and more pressure. From a theological perspective, she experienced an echo of what Paul meant when he wrote that "no one will be justified by the works of the law" and "if righteousness comes through the law, then Christ died for nothing" (Gal. 2:16, 21).

An external style of attribution, however, looks beyond the self for somebodyness. My mother doesn't love me because I'm always exceptional but because I'm hers. The algebra teacher listens to his students' questions so attentively because that's his job (and he's good at it), not because middle schoolers are particularly interesting. Our boss agreed to that initial job interview because he's friends with our folks, and they begged him for a favor. And so on.

Dignity and esteem are just the beginning. An external style of attribution applies to status as well. It comes into view whenever the source of our somebodyness lies outside of us and is not subject to our direct influence.

For instance, I have certain legal rights and stature because I was born in the United States, not because I learned to walk by a certain age. A more vivid example would be the one my brother John experienced after getting married to his wife, Sara Beth. Before they met, Sara Beth had spent much of her twenties traversing the globe. International travel was one of her chief passions in life, the goal behind

---

11. "Naomi Osaka Press Conference," 2021 US Open Round 3 press conference, posted by US Open Tennis Championships, September 4, 2021, YouTube, https://www.youtube.com/watch?v=9_g4izDqqwA.

every side hustle she took. As a result, Sara Beth accrued enough frequent flyer miles with Delta to qualify for platinum status. John, on the other hand, had pretty much stayed put in the years before they got together. He tells the story of showing up to JFK Airport for their honeymoon and seeing an extraordinarily long line of people waiting to check in. Ugh. To the right of the general line stood a desk marked "platinum status"—with zero travelers in front of it. He watched as Sara Beth walked in that direction and said, "Come with me."

"But I don't have platinum status," John said. "Only you do."

"Don't worry about it," Sara Beth said. The moment she gave the Delta employee her passport, they not only welcomed her by name, they asked for John's ticket. John watched as they delightedly processed his check-in. The miles belonged to Sara Beth but, out of love, she allowed him to be enveloped by her credentials. There was nothing fictious about it; all of a sudden, through no effort of his own, John was jetting around the world in style! Lucky guy.

Imputation Station

Christianity embraces the external style of attribution. And the word it uses to capture this gracious dynamic is *imputation*, which means "to ascribe qualities to someone that are not there intrinsically, to regard somebody as a person that he or she is not."[12] The word first emerged as a translation of the Greek word *logizomai* in Romans 4:3.[13] In his 1516 Latin translation of the New Testament, Erasmus of Rotterdam argues that the Latin word *imputare*, which was used in Roman law courts to refer to the verbal remission of debt, best captures the sense of *logizomai* in this verse. It was this usage that Philip Melanchthon picked up on in developing the concept of imputation in early Protestant theology.[14]

12. Paul F. M. Zahl, *Grace in Practice: A Theology of Everyday Life* (Eerdmans, 2007), 119.
13. "Abraham believed God, and it was reckoned [*elogisthē*] to him as righteousness."
14. See Alister McGrath, *Iustitia Dei: A History of the Christian Doctrine of Justification*, 4th ed. (Cambridge University Press, 2020), 209–10.

Originally, then, *imputation* is a term borrowed from the world of accounting. It may sound dry or antiseptic at first but becomes less so once you reflect on how much of our lives revolve around numbers: number of followers, number of votes, number of years old, numbers in a bank account, number of church members, and so on. Indeed, if atonement speaks to us inside the courtroom of life, then imputation has something to say to us when life takes on the quality of a balance sheet—when we cannot outrun what we owe others and they owe us. Imputation is of Big Relief to those who suspect they are living in the red.

Theologically, imputation represents an answer to a question that has plagued Christians since the church's inception. How might a good and holy God reconcile himself to sinful human beings? Aren't the two incompatible? A good God, after all, wouldn't be good if he turned a blind eye to the damage we do to one another.

One theory holds that God infuses sinners with his own goodness, making them righteous (or lovable) in the process. This approach—what we might call the infusion of righteousness—is a form of internal attribution.

Imputation proposes something different. It announces that God reconciles sinners to himself by declaring them to be righteous on account of Christ. That is to say, God does not judge you or me on the basis of our own actions or identities—our spiritual or moral résumés, as it were—but on the basis of Christ's, which, through his death and resurrection, have been imputed to us by faith. Our account has been settled. God does not have to do this; he does it for no other reason than he loves us. As one classic summary puts it, "Christ's merits are given to us so that we might be reckoned righteous by our trust in the merits of Christ when we believe in him, as though we had merits of our own."[15] You and I may grow in righteousness as a result of this imputation, or we may not; that,

15. Philipp Melanchthon, *Apology of the Augsburg Confession*, article 21 (1530), in *The Book of Concord (New Translation): The Confessions of the Evangelical Lutheran Church*, ed. Robert Kolb and Timothy J. Wengert (Fortress, 2000), 240.

too, is up to God. In a world drowning in status anxiety, it's hard to imagine a bigger relief.

After he won the Masters Tournament in 2024, professional golfer Scottie Scheffler drew on the doctrine of imputation in his post-championship press conference. He said,

> I was sitting around with my buddies this morning, and I was a bit overwhelmed. Because I wish I didn't want to win as badly as I do. I think it would make the mornings easier. But I love winning. I hate losing. I really do. . . . My buddies told me this morning that my victory was secure on the cross. That's a pretty special feeling. To know that I'm secure for forever. And it doesn't matter whether or not I win this tournament or I lose this tournament. My identity is secure forever.[16]

The external style of attribution did something remarkable that day. It granted Scheffler a measure of peace no matter the outcome, which is precisely what he needed to win. Imputation, by grounding our identity outside ourselves in the person and work of Jesus Christ, lends us not just comfort in challenging circumstances but the freedom to take risks in those circumstances. Unlike in an internal style of attribution, Scheffler's identity was not at stake, just the day's game. A belief in the God who imputes also appears to have lent Scheffler some genuine humility that day, as manifested in his refusal to take full credit for the victory.

Of course, as with all things grace related, we are a lot more open to the beauty of imputation when life is going poorly than when it is going well. When our personal stock is rising, the temptation to believe in our specialness—and other people's lack thereof—is strong. The tighter we cling to the status we feel we've earned, the more imputation will offend our pride.

Jesus's disciples are a case in point. Despite their proximity to Christ himself, they were not immune to status games. In fact, just

16. "The 2024 Masters Champion Scottie Scheffler Chronicles His Second Green Jacket Victory," press conference, posted by The Masters, April 14, 2024, YouTube, https://www.youtube.com/watch?v=sftys9JG7pc.

after the book of Mark reaches its dramatic midpoint on the Mount of Transfiguration, Jesus catches them in the act. They've made their way down the mountain and are heading through Galilee. Doubtless the glory they had just witnessed had rubbed off. I imagine there was a palpable sense not only of excitement but of self-congratulation on having hitched their wagons to the right star. "Then they came to Capernaum, and when [Jesus] was in the house he asked them, 'What were you arguing about on the way?' But they were silent, for on the way they had argued with one another about who was the greatest. He sat down, called the twelve, and said to them, 'Whoever wants to be first must be last of all and servant of all'" (Mark 9:33–35).

Ruh-roh. Jesus wastes no time in demolishing his disciples' less-than-holy understanding of status. The last shall be first in the kingdom of God, he tells them, before taking a child in his arms. Children in that society had no status. Contemporary attitudes about the innocence and preciousness of minors did not apply. Kids had no economic or political power. They occupied the bottom rung of the social and religious ladder. And yet, because they have no pretense of being valued according to their usefulness or personal righteousness, Jesus exalts them.[17] Little ones have no pride to prevent them from accepting the status he bestows on them, though they are undeserving. Jesus goes so far as to directly identify with children: "Whoever welcomes one such child in my name welcomes me" (Mark 9:37).

Who is the greatest in the kingdom of God? Not the person busy jockeying for esteem—or endlessly establishing their identity—but the one who has no choice but to receive those things from the God who gave them all up.

---

17. It is easy for contemporary audiences to miss the radicality of what Jesus is doing here. We live, after all, in an almost pathologically "child-forward" culture, where most parents' schedules are dictated by their children's activities (rather than the other way around), à la the cohort described at the opening of this chapter. My friend Sarah Condon, herself a mother to young children, jokes that modern parents "are like Amazon drivers—but our packages hate us." It's a funny characterization but perhaps less funny when you read reports from the US Surgeon General like the one issued in August 2024, warning that parental stress in the United States has reached unprecedented and near-critical levels. This report, titled "Parents Under Pressure," is available at https://www.hhs.gov/surgeongeneral/priorities/parents/index.html.

The How of Grace

Whenever we are shown love we do not deserve—when we are loved by someone right in the middle of our unlovability—we witness the power of imputation. It is what love looks like when the one being loved doesn't seem worthy of that affection. Imputation is, to borrow again from my brother John, the "how of grace."

It is no coincidence that John's second favorite movie of all time is the 1946 classic film *The Best Years of Our Lives*, directed by William Wyler.[18] The movie follows three World War II veterans as they return to the United States. Homer Parrish is a sailor who comes home having lost both of his hands to an explosion.[19] We learn that before he left, Homer got engaged to Wilma, the lovely daughter of the lifelong friends who live next door to his family. After returning, though, Homer avoids Wilma, ashamed of his disability and the prosthetic hooks that he now wears as hands. He is both mired in self-pity and convinced that if she were to see the reality of what his life has become, she would reject him. And so he takes the path of avoidance, hoping she'll get the message and move on. Wilma is not dissuaded. But she is also so distraught by Homer's distancing that her parents decide to send her away so that her broken heart can mend.

The night before her departure, she sees the light go on at Homer's house and decides to confront him. Homer answers the door in his bathrobe, his body language telegraphing deep resignation and sadness. Wilma tells Homer what her parents have planned, which he defeatedly affirms as a wise idea. Then Wilma tells him that she doesn't want to go, that she'd like more than anything to stay with him. The depressed veteran realizes that he can avoid the truth no longer and comes out with what he's been thinking. He says, "You don't know what it'd be like to have to live with me. To have to face

18. His top favorite might be even more a masterpiece of Big Relief, Akira Kurosawa's *Red Beard* (1965).

19. Homer is played by nonactor (and real-life disabled veteran) Harold Russell, who won an honorary Academy Award for the role.

this every day, every night . . . I'm going upstairs to bed—I want you to come up and see for yourself what happens."

"All right, Homer," Wilma says. She follows him up the stairs to his bedroom, where he takes off his robe to reveal the medieval-like prosthetic harness underneath. We watch as he removes straps and reveals his handless arms. He tells Wilma,

> I've learned how to take this harness off. I can wiggle into my pajama top. I'm lucky I have my elbows. Some of the boys don't. But I can't button [the pajamas] up. This is when I know I'm helpless. My hands are down there on the bed. I can't put them on again without calling someone for help. I can't smoke a cigarette or read a book. If that door should blow shut, I can't open it and get out of this room. As dependent as a baby that doesn't know how to do anything except cry for it.
>
> Well, now you know, Wilma. Now you have an idea of what it is. I guess you don't know what to say. It's all right. Go on home. Go away, like your family said.

Wilma is emotional but undaunted. She says, "I know what to say Homer. I love you. And I'm never going to leave you. Never." She then kisses him, passionately.

"You mean, you didn't mind?" Homer says, undone by her persistence.

"Of course not," Wilma says. "I told you I loved you."

Wilma puts away the prosthetics and helps the dumbstruck man into bed. She then turns off the light and closes the door, leaving him lying there, tears streaming down his face. I cry along with Homer every time I watch. And I keep crying all through the next scene, in which the couple gets married in Wilma's living room. When Homer appears on camera, he's smiling from ear to ear, his countenance completely transformed. He's been made whole by the power of his wife-to-be's imputing love.[20]

20. *The Best Years of Our Lives*, directed by William Wyler (Samuel Goldwyn, 1946).

Homer's accident hadn't just maimed him. It had blinded him. Yet what matters is how Wilma sees Homer, not how Homer sees himself. Wilma treats him as if he were something he isn't—not in that moment, surely. She sees past the defective charity case he believes himself to be and imputes to him an altogether different identity, that of an honorable man worth building a life with. In that moment Homer is reborn. This is what we mean when we talk about imputation as the how of grace. Wilma's devotion hints at what Martin Luther meant when he wrote, "The love of God does not find, but creates, that which is pleasing to it."[21]

Put in more gut-level terms, you and I are not loved by God because we are special. We are special because we are loved by God. The attribution is external; it depends on God, not us. Our status, our identity, and our value are secure in Christ and, therefore, not dependent on our waxing and waning performance in school or golf or even discipleship. As Philip Yancey once wrote, "Grace means there is nothing we can do to make God love us more. And grace means there is nothing we can do to make God love us less."[22] What Big Relief for Homers everywhere.

Your thing, in other words, is not that you're good at tennis or growing yams, delicious as they may be. Your thing is that you are a beloved child of God.

21. Martin Luther, *Luther's Works*, vol. 31, *Career of the Reformer I*, ed. Jaroslav Jan Pelikan, Hilton C. Oswald, and Helmut T. Lehmann (Fortress, 1999), 57.
22. Philip Yancey, *What's So Amazing about Grace?* (Zondervan, 1997), 70.

7

Rest

The Relief from Keeping Up

I knew with 100 percent certainty what he would say. I just didn't know how long it would take for him to say it.

My son had begged me to put on an episode of *The Twilight Zone* that he had heard his grandfather rave about. It's an episode called "The After Hours," an eerie tale about mannequins that come to life in a department store. It originally aired in 1960 and was filmed in black and white.

About three minutes in, he started to fidget. This was not remarkable, as he was ten years old. But the fidgeting soon blossomed into full-blown agitation. Around the five-minute mark he came out with it: "Dad, why is it so *slow*?" This is the same comment he made when we watched *It's a Wonderful Life* a few months prior. It wasn't that he didn't understand what was going on or find it interesting. But the pace threw him off.

The shows he usually consumed were much more quickly paced: more cuts, less dialogue, more action. *Shows* might actually be a misnomer, since his favorite thing to watch was YouTube Shorts, which are sixty-second bursts of video content piled one on top of the other, algorithmically tailored to make sure no one looks away.

111

We parents told ourselves it was better than TikTok with its fifteen-second videos. While some of the stuff was clever, most of it was inane, an example of what is increasingly referred to as the "dopamine culture" that has taken over our collective imagination.[1]

My son wasn't the only one starting to feel antsy as Rod Serling wove his tale. I could feel the pull of the phone in my pocket. This would be an easy show to watch while scrolling through something or other, as I had fallen into the habit of doing. The "two-screen experience," I've heard it called.

The common explanation for our shared agitation has to do with shrinking attention spans. Kids today just can't focus on anything for more than a few seconds at a time. I heard the same refrain from adults when I was growing up. Perhaps this is true; it's hard to say for certain. Few ten-year-old boys I've known have been adept at concentration. What can be said, however, is that the pace of entertainment has greatly accelerated since "The After Hours" first aired.

Acceleration is the key word here, and television is merely the tip of the iceberg. Theologian Andrew Root, paraphrasing sociologist Hartmut Rosa, defines *modernity* as "the constant process of speeding things up."[2] We experience this acceleration in too many spheres to count. Technology, for instance, continually makes communication faster. Letters become phone calls, which become emails, which become texts, which become real-time Slack messages, and so on. Each new update to our local network doubles connection

1. "Dopamine culture" is a term coined by writer Ted Gioia to describe how distraction has supplanted entertainment as the animating force behind contemporary popular culture. Sometime in the past decade or so, he observes, attention that was trained on television shows shifted to video clips and then to reels. In music, consumers (and artists) largely abandoned albums as their preferred medium and pursued the more commercial possibilities of tracks and then hooks. "Dopamine culture," he writes, "is based on body chemistry, not fashion or aesthetics. Our brain rewards these brief bursts of distraction. The neurochemical dopamine is released, and this makes us feel good—so we want to repeat the stimulus" ("The State of Culture, 2024," The Honest Broker, February 18, 2024, https://www.honest-broker.com/p/the-state-of-the-culture-2024). If it sounds a bit like chemical dependency, well, the shoe fits.
2. Andrew Root, *The Congregation in a Secular Age: Keeping Sacred Time against the Speed of Modern Life* (Baker Academic, 2021), 14.

speed. Meanwhile, drawers fill up with discarded old cords we're convinced may someday come in handy. Our devices—and their many chargers—become obsolete at shorter and shorter intervals.

The economy also accelerates year after year. Markets rise and fall, but prices never really drop, as consumers pay heretofore unimagined sums for used cars and houses and groceries. "Every year we have to run a bit faster to keep what we have" is how Rosa describes the pressure that acceleration places on us.[3]

Then there's the job market. When I started working with undergraduate college students in 2010, I was surprised to see how many of them applied for postcollege jobs during the fall of their junior year. Internships during the final summer of college were a foregone conclusion for anyone interested in joining a big corporation. This had not been the case when I was at university the previous decade. By 2016 the timetable had shifted, and that same application process now took place during spring of sophomore year. By the time I stepped back from student ministry in 2023, the most career-driven kids had secured an offer before they began their freshman year.

The pace of social change seems to quicken too. I remember reading a 2018 interview with actor Steve Carell in which he suggested that *The Office* couldn't be made anymore because the humor was outdated.[4] The show had only gone off the air in 2013, but cultural sensitivities—particularly around gender and race—had evolved so quickly that he thought the humor would no longer fly.

Then there's political acceleration. A friend remarked to me recently that he'd fallen out with a former roommate during the Bush–Kerry presidential race of 2004. The moment he said it, we both chuckled in disbelief. The emotional tenor of that election seems so quaint in comparison to the histrionics of campaigns today.

3. He calls this process "dynamic stabilization." Thijs Lijster, Robin Celikates, and Hartmut Rosa, "Beyond the Echo-Chamber: An Interview with Hartmut Rosa on Resonance and Alienation," *Krisis | Journal for Contemporary Philosophy* 39, no. 1 (2019): 64–78, https://doi.org/10.21827/krisis.39.1.37365.

4. Bruce Handy, "Mensch at Work," *Esquire*, October 11, 2018, https://www.esquire.com/entertainment/movies/a23695483/steve-carell-beautiful-boy-interview-2018/.

I could keep going. The overall picture I'm trying to paint is of life as a treadmill on which the dial keeps moving upward. We all feel it. The fast track keeps getting faster, our need for relief that much more urgent.

Exhaustion Fatigue

The fruit of all this acceleration is manifold. Three byproducts worth highlighting are anxiety, alienation, and fatigue.

As the pace of life ratchets up, so, too, does our anxiety. It can't not. The more we try to accomplish in less time, the more it feels like we're losing control over our own lives and the world. The train could go off its tracks at any moment when you're moving this fast, and that's a fear-inducing prospect. High-speed crashes tend to be fatal, after all. Less time also means less agency. Reflection starts to feel like a luxury we cannot afford while we're barreling from one thing to the next. Our options in any given situation constrain to whatever we can swing on the fly. This is not a recipe for spiritual well-being, which tends to be cultivated through prayer and meditation and the sort of fellowship with others that hurry disallows. Serenity is never frenzied.

It is not just the pace of activity that accelerates, by the way, but the volume. I mean that in both senses of the word. An accelerating world is an increasingly noisy world. We are all broadcasters now if we'd like to be. Visit a members-only lounge in any airport, and you'll find a room full of worn-out travelers paying a premium for silence. When I was in elementary school, certain parents sounded the alarm about television turning their kids' brains to mush. It was too much stimulation, they said, information overload. They had no idea what was coming.[5] If you've ever been on a plane with a screaming baby, you know that as the decibels rise, so does your blood pressure.

5. And we don't either!

114

Acceleration exacerbates the pressure to keep up, which feels harder and harder. This is more than just keeping up with the Joneses. We have to keep up with our inboxes, our bills, our bodies, our friendships, our commitments. Thus, we anxiously run around, trying in vain to stay on top of things and feeling all the while that everyone else is ahead of us.

The inevitable consequence of that pressure is the second fallout, alienation. Journalist Anne Helen Petersen sums up the everyday experience of acceleration like this: "Most people feel left behind in some way—no matter what their life is like. Parents feel like their friends without kids have left them behind and are flaky. Kid-free people feel like their parent friends only want to hang out with other parents and are also flaky. Parents feel like society is incredibly hostile to them; single people feel like society is incredibly hostile to them; partnered people without kids feel like society is incredibly hostile to them."[6]

I could add any number of groups to her list. Old people, young people, conservative people, liberal people, religious people, blue-collar people (especially men!), and yes, even wealthy people feel like they're being left behind.[7] The fear of being left behind is ubiquitous, and not just in the end-time connotation of that phrase. When the world moves on without us, we believe it renders us irrelevant. We equate being left behind with being discarded and less-than, yesterday's news. To keep up is to remain in the game, vital and valued. Being left behind represents a negative verdict that we scurry like mad to avoid.

Petersen hints at an underlying truth that is getting harder to ignore. A society that must accelerate to perpetuate itself soon

6. Anne Helen Petersen, "How to Show Up for Your Friends without Kids—and How to Show Up for Kids and Their Parents," *Culture Study*, July 20, 2022, https://annehelen.substack.com/p/how-to-show-up-for-your-friends-without.

7. Having logged significant hours in wealthy enclaves as a youth minister, I can testify that the anxiety about "downward social mobility"—a.k.a. the sense that the world has passed the former ruling class by and that the old rules no longer apply—is palpable. See also, Whit Stillman's terrific 1989 film *Metropolitan*.

becomes hostile to humanity, in part because humans slow down as we age. We are not machines that can be endlessly upgraded. I cannot move as fast as I did when I was twenty-five. No one can, not even Tom Brady.

Very often, this hostility manifests as alienation or the loss of connection. You cannot feel connected to your surroundings, especially the other people in your surroundings, if you do not have the time to invest in them. Acceleration pinches our available minutes, and often the first activities to get the axe are those that don't bring an immediate or quantifiable return. These tend to be the same activities that yield the most connection.[8]

When my kids were little, we lived in a neighborhood that hosted Fourth of July and Halloween parades. These events were some of the highlights of our year. And yet when the family who had organized them aged out, there was considerable consternation about whether the gatherings would continue. None of the younger families were willing to step forward, and I count my own in that number. It wasn't that we didn't value the parades—we came out in droves!—but the idea of putting anything more, especially something nonmandatory, onto our already crowded plates was too overwhelming to contemplate.

The truth is, we feel connected to a community to the extent that we're able to both receive from *and* give to it. Acceleration squashes the amount of energy we're able to offer our church, our schools, our swim teams, and the result is that even if we stay involved, we're there mainly as consumers, not contributors.

The Ministry of Napping

The third fallout of all this acceleration is exhaustion, and as with anxiety, you don't have to look far to find the evidence. Adolescents aren't getting enough sleep. College students are wiped out. Teachers

8. Hint: rhymes with *burch*!

are barely standing. Your mail carrier is snowed under. Every clergy-person I know needs a sabbatical. Activists are running out of gas. Men in their fifties are burned out. Women in their forties too. The high schoolers I know decry "the overwhelm." Most of the retirees in my orbit are constantly dozing off. Everyone is tired. The only question is what we're tired from. We're even tired of the word *tired* and burned out on the term *burnout*. We talk instead about fatigue, whether that be compassion fatigue, political fatigue, Zoom fatigue, crisis fatigue, inflation fatigue, or dress-up-as-Taylor-Swift-day-at-my-kids'-school fatigue. You get the idea.

Religion is not immune to acceleration. Churches often fall prey to the assumption that growth—personal, communal, institutional—is the be-all and end-all of what happens on Sundays. In trying to remain relevant, well-meaning staff add new programs and services and supercharge existing ones.[9] We develop apps that allow people to get their devotions done more quickly and conveniently. We film video curricula that make it possible for teenagers to prep for confirmation while out of town at a hockey game. We host tongue-sorta-in-cheek booths for drive-by ashes on Ash Wednesday.

At its best, however, the church is meant to resist acceleration. The very notion of a weekly Sabbath breaks the twenty-four-seven cycle of *more* and reminds us that we are God's treasured children, not slaves to the ever-mounting demands of the pharaohs in our lives. Once we walk through its doors, the church often feels out of time, its rituals and modalities (and carpets!) unchanged in hundreds of years. At least in the liturgical tradition in which I grew up, services are not fast-paced. They sometimes seem intentionally, even aggressively, boring—a facet that drove me crazy as a kid but I now crave as an adult. I don't mean that I crave pastors speaking in monotone or dragging out the announcements until everyone's eyes glaze over. What I crave are the pauses, the comfortable silences, an overall rhythm that doesn't mimic the manic tone of YouTube and

---

9. Alas, volunteer fatigue is a thing, as is donor fatigue.

TikTok and instead allows a person space to breathe. The slowness itself is a relief.

Then again, maybe falling asleep in church wouldn't be the end of the world. Cue Tricia Hersey, founder of The Nap Ministry. In response to the more dehumanizing aspects of grind culture—about which she says, "We are praised and rewarded for ignoring our body's need for rest, care, and repair"—Hersey has spent several years staging what she calls "collective napping experiences" around the country.[10] Part performance art, part political activism, part spiritual healing, these napping experiences invite strangers to shut their eyes in public, lying down next to one another on pillows and yoga mats. Harps are sometimes involved, as are soothing playlists and guided relaxation techniques, all geared toward encouraging people to embrace what Hersey calls their "divine right to rest." To be made in God's image is to be a person who needs rest. Inevitably someone wakes up crying, explaining how profound it feels to give themselves permission to rest.

While Hersey does not characterize The Nap Ministry as specifically Christian, in her book *Rest Is Resistance*, she explains how the project is grounded in Black liberation theology, as well as in her own roots in the Pentecostal denomination Church of God in Christ. She credits teachers like James Cone with instilling in her the conviction that "I was not born to simply exhaust myself inside a violent system. I know that if I never check another item off my to-do list, I am still worthy and loved by God and my Ancestors."[11] This notion, that God values us apart from our output and invites us to rest in his love, draws on a framework of grace—which is to say, it draws on the framework of Jesus.

Jesus rested all the time. When a storm raged on the Sea of Galilee and his disciples started to panic, they found Jesus napping in the front of the boat. He was a little irritated when they woke him but proceeded to calm the storm despite their frantic faithlessness. Jesus also never succumbed to hurry—sometimes to the detriment

10. Tricia Hersey, *Rest Is Resistance: A Manifesto* (Hachette Book Group, 2022), 32.
11. Hersey, *Rest Is Resistance*, 74–75.

of those in need of healing. Very early in Mark's Gospel, before Jesus has had a chance to do much of anything, he withdraws to a deserted place to pray. Jesus takes a deliberate pause from healing the sick and casting out demons: "In the morning, while it was still very dark, [Jesus] got up and went out to a deserted place, and there he prayed. And Simon and his companions hunted for him. When they found him, they said to him, 'Everyone is searching for you.' He answered, 'Let us go on to the neighboring towns, so that I may proclaim the message there also, for that is what I came out to do'" (Mark 1:35–38).

The pattern of the spiritual life, if we take Christ as our model, is not one of nonstop engagement. It involves regular retreat. The disciples do not follow this same pattern. Worry prompts them to seek out their teacher the moment he goes missing. And so they interrupt Jesus's prayers; they get in the way of his time with God. "Everyone is searching for you," they say with unintended irony. Yet Jesus does not meet them with a rebuke or with a rejection. He does not mirror their anxiety, nor does he give them a lecture about deceleration. No doubt he knew that shouting at people to slow down will not work any better than shouting at them to stop being sick. Instead, he responds with kindness and renewed focus.

Jesus, it turns out, does not want to be distracted from preaching the gospel. That's where his energy lies: in spreading the news that God has interrupted—and will continue to interrupt—the panicked pattern of the world. And he interrupts our to-and-fro not with a new form of spiritual grind but with the resonance and assurance of the Big Relief.

Resonance Restores

Retreating in the way Jesus did is usually a good idea. Sadly, acceleration runs so deep in our veins that relaxation alone cannot provide lasting comfort. I remember reading a study a few years ago that said that the number one thing you can do for your health is get good sleep. Eating well and exercising are important, but not as much as getting eight hours of shut-eye every night. Alas, a culture of acceleration (made up of you and me) transmutes this knowledge into marketing in the blink of an eye. Before we know it, we're being inundated with weighted face masks, white noise machines, and memory foam–spring coil hybrid mattresses to optimize our rest. Sleep becomes something at which we need to excel. It turns stressful.[12]

The same can be true with fatigue. Such is our wiring—culturally and individually—that we turn fatigue into a competitive sport. Writing in the *New Yorker* back in 1995, Betsy Berne observes, "I've noticed recently that the main topic of conversation among my friends is tiredness. Actually, there is an underlying contest over who is more tired and who has truly earned his or her tiredness."[13] Of course, life is not a struggle contest, and the extent to which we understand it to be so will be the extent to which we view others as competitors rather than as shoulders to lean on. Alienation will only abound.

The problems of acceleration—anxiety, alienation, and exhaustion—cannot be solved by maximizing relaxation any more than the problems of control can be solved by better technique. But that doesn't mean there isn't an answer. What we require, according to Hartmut Rosa, are experiences of "resonance."

Resonance is yet another one of those enigmatic words. Rosa defines it as "a mode of relating to the world in which the subject feels touched, moved, or addressed by the people, places, objects, etc., he or she encounters."[14] Resonant experiences are concrete experiences

12. A related phenomenon would be "orthosomnia," which is obsessing over getting good rest to the extent that we lose sleep worrying about it. Of course, the beautiful thing about sleep is that once you've passed out, it doesn't really matter how or why you got there. Sleep takes us, not vice versa.

13. Betsy Berne, "The Tired Chronicles," *New Yorker*, July 30, 1995, https://www.newyorker.com/magazine/1995/08/07/the-tired-chronicles. She goes on, "According to the tired married people with kids, there is no contest. They are the royalty of the tired kingdom. They are smug with exhaustion." Feel free to kiss the ring.

14. Hartmut Rosa, "The Idea of Resonance as a Sociological Concept," *Global Dialogue*, July 9, 2018, https://globaldialogue.isa-sociology.org/articles/the-idea-of-resonance-as-a-sociological-concept.

in which we are drawn out of our heads, which is to say, out of projection about the future and into the present. Sometimes this occurs through beauty—taking in a sunset, for instance. Sometimes it occurs through story, such as watching a movie that strikes a deep and unexpected emotional chord. Art is a common avenue for resonance.

The most resonant experience I had last year occurred at a rock concert. For our anniversary, my wife bought us tickets to see singer Peter Gabriel. I was delighted when she told me but had also been a superfan long enough to harbor some trepidation. Gabriel hadn't toured the United States in decades, and the energy to pull off an arena show requires the stamina typical of a man half his age. I knew I'd get a kick out of seeing my hero in person, but I didn't want to burst the bubble of admiration by witnessing a subpar show. Never meet your heroes, right?

Fortunately, from the moment Gabriel opened his mouth—and the accompanying art installation flickered on—all sense of time and place vanished. I felt profoundly and personally addressed by what was happening, as though the songs had been written just for me. For two and a half hours, the world felt animated and alive, and I was buzzing within it, right where I should be. It wasn't so much a feeling of transcendence—of being above or outside of time—but of residing fully within time. For the first encore, Gabriel trotted out his immortal love song "In Your Eyes," which contains the couplet, "I get so tired of working so hard for our survival / I look to the time with you to keep me awake and alive."[15] Looking back, I realize we were having a resonant experience listening to a song about resonance, in this case, the experience of falling in love. As we drove home, despite having been up for hours, I felt more refreshed than I had in months.

Part of what makes experiences of resonance so powerful is that they are, by definition, not subject to our engineering. We may

15. Peter Gabriel, "In Your Eyes," track 5 on *So*, Charisma, 1986.

purchase the tickets, or press play on Spotify, but resonance moves *toward* us, with a power all its own. As Rosa notes, experiences of resonance are those that act upon us—we are spoken to *by* a sermon, moved *by* a painting, grabbed *by* an interest—rather than those we design for ourselves. Resonance occurs when a child does something unexpected while we're playing with them, and it delights us in such a way that we are pulled into the moment. Resonance reminds us that the world is rich with meaning and that meaning exists independently of our attempts to control or manufacture or even recognize it. Andrew Root expounds on resonance when he writes,

> When we sense that there is something in the world reaching out for us, pleased to join us, desiring to share in us as we share in it, speaking to us, we encounter resonance. We feel not like we're speeding on the surface of the world but connected to the world and those in it. In these moments, time is felt not as accelerating but as full. . . . Time is no longer speeding past us, the currents of modernity forcing us out of the present. In resonance we rest in the good of the present. We rest in the good of just being alive, of having this full moment of feeling connected (to our own bodies, to a friend, to a God who sees and sends).[16]

We feel resonance, in other words, to the extent we feel connected to the world and ourselves—but not just any connection or any world. Resonance depends on us not being responsible for the connection in question. It must have come *to* us, yanking us out of our planning and managing and worrying. Moreover, the world to which we feel connected cannot be a frightful or imposing one. In moments of resonance, we sense only its welcome.

This means that experiences of God are always resonant. After all, we believe that God meets us, not the other way around. We do not sing "I once was lost, but then I found God" but "I once was lost but now *am* found [by God]." The Big Relief—which we could

16. Root, *Congregation in a Secular Age*, 196.

just as well call the Big Resonance—maintains that God does the seeking and the finding; you and I are the lost sheep in the equation. Indeed, in the measured pace of a (good) church service we remember the incarnation of a creator who refuses to remain aloof from his creation but, like an octopus, punctures the bubble of alienation to which we so often retreat in our pain. And God doesn't puncture with ill intent. He descends Jacob's ladder in love to muddy himself with the cares and concerns of everyday people. In other words, God comes to us with grace, drawing us deeper into the world he made, which he called good. When Christians say the Hound of Heaven tracked them down with merciful determination and gifted them with belonging and purpose, they are describing an experience of deep resonance.

Not surprisingly, encounters with Jesus during his lifetime did not speed by but followed a peculiar rhythm. They were the sort of encounters a person spent the rest of their life telling others about, moments of connection when time evaporated and God's loving attention eclipsed all other concerns. In reading the Gospels, one surmises that to be gazed upon by the eyes of Jesus was to glimpse not only the light and the heat but, as Gabriel sings, "the doorway to a thousand churches."[17]

Blessed Assurance

There is another element to the rest that God grants weary souls caught in the trap of acceleration. In addition to retreat and resonance, the Big Relief includes a message of assurance.

Broadly speaking, assurance is the confidence that God's grace applies to you and me. Assurance guarantees that grace is big enough to cover (even) you, come what may. This differs from the grace we experience when we're given permission to get off the treadmill, as well as the grace we experience when we encounter resonance—both

17. This is also from the song "In Your Eyes."

of which are beautiful but temporary. We awake from naps, after all. The delight we feel when holding a baby expires when they get fussy and tired themselves (or become teenagers).

If retreat addresses our fatigue, and resonance alleviates our alienation, then perhaps assurance speaks to our anxiety. It contains a finality we can lean on.

What I mean is that in an accelerating world, demand never ceases. There is always one more email to return, one more headline to absorb, one more update to our phone's software, one more Zoom to dial in to, one more pile of leaves to rake, one more application to turn in, one more bill to pay, one more meal to cook, one more dish to wash, one more family gathering to plan, one more apology to make, one more tirade to endure, one more excuse to give, one more excuse to listen to—one more thing to do until we reach Enough.

Acceleration ensures that whatever threshold we're chasing only gets further and further away. It makes me think of the Letter to the Hebrews, in which the writer speaks of priests "offering again and again the same sacrifices that can never take away sins" (10:11). These priests cannot appease God. Each fresh sacrifice yields to the next: one more, then one more, then one more. Bigger, stronger, faster.

The writer then says something remarkable: "But when Christ had offered for all time a single sacrifice for sins, 'he sat down at the right hand of God'" (10:12). He sat down. Done. No more appeasement necessary. When it comes to God, nothing that needs to be done has not been done. This assurance is impervious to loss. That is, like the weathered old bench on the cover of this book, the relief Jesus offers anxious sinners is both solid and permanent.

God is not another accelerant. When the soldiers come to arrest Jesus in the garden of Gethsemane, he refuses to run. Then, when Pilate interrogates him the next day, Jesus does not ramp up the noise but remains silent, opting to bear the full brunt of Rome's coldhearted efficiency. Even his resurrection isn't hurried. His body lies lifeless in the tomb for three days. When he rises from the grave, instead of rushing to the ascension, he lingers. The disciples who scattered when he was crucified and were left behind don't have to run to catch up. Instead, Jesus catches up to them—cooking breakfast over charcoal as the fishing boats slowly dock. He meets them and us where we are. With him, even those who have been left behind have not in fact been left behind.

8

Play

The Relief from Productivity

Sock Wars is not a complicated game. That's probably why it was such a favorite. First, you need to clear a decent-sized room, preferably one that's carpeted. Next, everyone takes off their shoes. The goal of the game is to keep your socks on, and the only real rule is that you're not allowed to get on your feet. Most people move around on their knees, which has a way of evening the playing field. The last person with at least one sock on wins.

As you might expect, the game degenerates into a melee pretty quickly. No one was ever (seriously) hurt on our watch, thank God.

Another favorite game was lights-out hide-and-seek. A few injuries *did* result from this one, but fewer than you'd think. If we had known about Human Hungry Hippos—the game where partners slide each other around on dollies, stomach down, while the human "hippos" attempt to grab as many balloons as possible—no doubt that would have made the list as well.

The "they" in question were the middle school boys who attended the Bible study that my friend Drake and I ran in West Hartford, Connecticut, for about three years in the mid-2000s. His younger brother, John, was a seventh grader, and their church didn't have much going on in the youth group department. John enlisted us to organize something and invited his friends. A group of ten to twenty of them routinely showed up on Monday afternoons.

The format of the meetings was simple: pile into the basement for thirty minutes of games, break for fifteen minutes of pizza, during which everyone shared their "high and low" of the week, and close with five to seven minutes of God talk and a brief prayer. Now that I have a thirteen-year-old boy of my own, I think about those days often. There was more magic in that basement than we realized at the time.

I doubt the same format would work today. In fact, I know it wouldn't. The travel sports and college admissions industrial complexes have annexed too large a share of middle school afternoons. There is no way to rationalize Sock Wars as a résumé enhancer. No one would mistake it for a productive use of time. Human Hungry Hippos does not develop any marketable skills.

Yet isn't that the trouble? In the fifteen years since we held those meetings, fun has become a harder sell—at least if the context in which my wife and I are raising our family is any indication.[1] It's not that we like fun less than we used to, but parents and children feel pressure, by middle school if not earlier, to make the most of post-school hours. Extracurriculars must contribute to personal growth. We cannot afford to waste them on useless hilarity. They must be *productive.*

Don't get me wrong. Our kids aren't forced to work in factories. They're not living in a gray-clad Orwellian dystopia. They still have plenty of occasion for fun. But the quickest way to get parents to sign off on that fun is if there's some discernible purpose to it, preferably one related to growth or achievement. Enjoyment alone isn't sufficient.

I think of a couple I met at the pool who boasted about their son playing Minecraft for hours on end because he's purportedly honing skills that he might use as an architect one day. The other day I overheard

1. A fairly affluent corner of the coastal United States in the 2020s.

an acquaintance justifying the astronomical sum of money she spent on Taylor Swift tickets for her daughter on the grounds of Taylor's economic dominance and general #Girlbossness. She thought it was important for her daughter to witness a successful woman achieving her dreams, that it might inspire her daughter to do the same. All well and good, of course, but she could've mentioned that a dance party of such epic proportions is a once-in-a-lifetime blast for all involved, or that it would simply fulfill the desire of the young girl's heart.

I fear that for middle schoolers, fun for fun's sake has been either relegated to birthday parties—prone to an acceleration of their own—or outsourced to YouTubers like Mr. Beast.[2]

It's not just adolescents who aren't having fun. Early adulthood, conventionally considered the apex of good times, has become a period of protracted anxiety and depression for more and more of us. Weddings, birthday parties, and summer vacations are as exhausting as they are expensive.[3] The 2022 American Time Use Survey revealed a precipitous decline across all demographics in the amount of time Americans spend socializing or simply hanging out. From 2003 to 2022, the average hours that American men spent face-to-face socializing declined by about 30 percent. The decrease for unmarried Americans was even larger—more than 35 percent. But teenagers experienced the most dramatic shift. They experienced a *45 percent* decrease in in-person socializing during those years. In other words, girls and boys between the ages of fifteen and nineteen reduced their weekly hangout time by more than three hours per week. These declines began well before the advent of smartphones and the COVID-19 pandemic.[4]

2. My hunch is that this trend represents a major opportunity for church youth groups the world over. A place that majors on fun of the most inane and gratuitous variety—where kids can be kids free of the pressure to produce or perform—will only become more precious in years to come. To speak of God in such a context only ups the potency.

3. The Knot reported that the average wedding in 2023 cost $304 per guest. Kim Forrest, "How Much Does the Average Wedding Cost, according to Data?," The Knot, February 19, 2024, https://www.theknot.com/content/average-wedding-cost.

4. Derek Thompson, "Why Americans Suddenly Stopped Hanging Out," *Atlantic*, February 14, 2024, https://www.theatlantic.com/ideas/archive/2024/02/america-decline-hanging-out/677451/.

The numbers track not only with the increase in self-reported lone-liness but with the overall impoverishment of fun described above. What is going on? We could blame the proliferation of screens and the Instagramization of culture, which has made leisure increasingly performative. Ostensibly fun activities like waterskiing or sledding become grist for the social media mill. It's not enough to have fun— you must have the *most* fun (and look good while doing so).

Alternately, we could blame the culture of fear that has engulfed nearly every aspect of middle-class parenting. Just run a straw poll of how many parents feel comfortable letting their children walk home from school by themselves, let alone spend the afternoon at the local playground unsupervised. I love my mom and dad, but the best times I had as a kid were almost always in the company of peers, not adults. They were certainly not at the direction of an adult.

Historically speaking, Christians have not been known for their fun. Growing up, I remember a friend describing his uptight, reli-gious mother as being perpetually worried that "someone some-where might be having too much fun." A fun-police outlook is the natural result of any religion that has personal growth rather than grace at its center.

Default on Your Productivity Debt

Ultimately, what we're dealing with here is the pressure of produc-tivity. This pressure has an economic dimension, related to the ac-celeration described in the previous chapter. Time is too precious to be squandered on activities that do not concretely develop our personalities. Frivolity feels superfluous to the point of, well, sinful-ness. But this pressure also has a spiritual dimension. It betrays an atrophying capacity for imagining ourselves apart from measurable accomplishment and work. Author Oliver Burkeman puts his finger on this pressure: "I would like to remind you (and also myself) that you don't start each morning in a kind of 'productivity debt' that you have to struggle to pay off through the day, in the hope of reaching a zero balance by the evening."[5]

When I read Burkeman's words to my wife, she couldn't stifle her guffaw. I have a habit, you see, of calling her on the phone most days around 4:30 p.m. I'll cloak the call in the excuse of inquiring about dinner, asking if there's anything I can pick up on the way home. But we've been married long enough that she knows why I'm really calling: I want to rattle off the day's achievements. I need to feel like I've gotten enough done to warrant a break. We laugh about it, but it's more than a little pathological. "Dave," she'll warmly say, "you know you're allowed to keep breathing even if you had an unproductive day?" I know this in my head, but it doesn't always reach my heart. She's a patient woman, my wife.

Of course, this pressure doesn't just apply to work. If I can't get enough done at the office, at least I can move the needle at home by being a productive husband, parent, son, or lawn-care specialist. If I can't contribute much there, there's always the task of making the world, or just my local community, a better place. There's so much to do to get to that zero balance Burkeman mentions. And just in case you're unsure of where you stand, we now have all sorts of metrics you can consult, from step counts and word counts, to weekly phone reports, to websites that log how many books you read annually.[6]

The pressure of productivity turns life into an enormous balance sheet, albeit one where nothing balances, and the accountants are continually cooking the books (or pulling their hair out). Grace flips things on their head. Burkeman entertained such an inversion when he posed several hypotheticals in reference to his original post: "What if you worked on the basis that you *began* each day at zero balance, so that everything you accomplished—every task you got

5. Oliver Burkeman, "What If You're Already on Top of Things?," *Oliver Burkeman* (blog), https://www.oliverburkeman.com/donelist.

6. No wonder the abuse of the prescription drug Adderall has become such a problem on college campuses. Instead of dropping ecstasy to "roll" with euphoria the way students did when I was in college, we now bend the law to increase our focus and productivity.

done, every tiny thing you did to address the world's troubles, or the needs of your household—put you ever further into the black? What if there's nothing you *ever* have to do to earn your spot on the planet? What if everything you actually get around to doing, on any given day, is in some important sense surplus?"[7]

What if, indeed! It all sounds very nice, but to ask these questions in earnest, I imagine you would have to adopt an entirely fresh basis of accounting. It sounds almost illegal.

Two Words Are Better Than Three

One of the chief ways that Christianity remains an engine of grace, and therefore relief, is the distinction it makes between the law and the gospel. This distinction has commonly been attributed to Martin Luther, but it goes back to Augustine and Paul before him, who was, of course, taking his cue from Jesus. The idea here is that God speaks in two words: *law* and *gospel*. The law tells us what we ought to do; the gospel tells us what God has done. The law shows us that we need to be forgiven; the gospel announces we *have been* forgiven. What sounds elementary often proves to be anything but.

When we think of the law in religious terms, most of us think of the Ten Commandments and the Sermon on the Mount: don't steal, don't murder, don't worship idols, love God with all your heart. This law, what I would call "Law with a capital *L*," gives shape to righteousness. It colors in the details of what Christians mean when they talk about right and wrong. These codes are daunting enough that anyone who approaches them honestly will walk away humbled, if not discouraged.

Luther recognized that the law also referred to an overarching spiritual principle of life in the world—a kind of elemental force that we experience every day. The law is present wherever we experience

7. Burkeman, "What If You're Already on Top of Things?" (emphasis added).

accusation and constraint and control and condemnation. This means that the law is at work on us even when we aren't hearing specific divine commands or thou-shalt-nots. For example, the internalized injunction around productivity that Burkeman references is an expression of what we might call "little-l law." You're almost always in its domain when you encounter an if-then construction: if I get enough done during the day, then I will be able to feel okay about myself. This is no different in impact than the more overtly religious notion that if we stay pure, then we will be accepted. *If* we follow God's commands, *then* we will secure God's favor. In each case, the law is the means by which we arrive at another end. It is instrumental at its core. We (attempt to) fulfill it in order to receive redemption, not because we delight in the commands themselves. We might even resent them.

Luther claimed that the law is "a constant guest" in our conscience.[8] What he meant was that the law is the air we breathe as human beings, our default setting. This sounds oppressive—and it is!—but we gravitate toward the law because of the control it promises. If I can just do x, y, or z, then I will get the result I want. If I can just be a certain kind of person, or project that persona publicly, then I will be loved. If I can just reach a zero balance in the productivity balance sheet, then I will matter at last. The problem of course, is that no one follows the law perfectly—not the little-*l* law of productivity and certainly not the capital-*L* Law of God.[9] How else to account for the fact that the most accomplished people feel more, rather than less, pressure to succeed?[10] The law commands, it reveals, it condemns, it categorizes, but it never comforts. It never delivers or saves. In fact, it often inspires rebellion.

8. Martin Luther, *Luther's Works*, vol. 26, *Lectures on Galatians, 1535, Chapters 1–4*, ed. Jaroslav Jan Pelikan, Hilton C. Oswald, and Helmut T. Lehmann (Fortress, 1999), 117.

9. See Jesus's interaction with the rich young ruler in Mark 10:17–22.

10. The upper-middle-class students at high-achieving schools discussed in chapter 6 (and their Ivy League counterparts) certainly fit this mold, but so do many folks who get to the top of their field. The 2024 Netflix docuseries *Simone Biles Rising* provides a particularly fascinating case in point, tracing how this dynamic has played out in the life of the legendary gymnast.

What a relief that God speaks a second word, the word of *gospel* or *good news*. News is not command. Command takes the imperative voice ("Do this"), but news takes the indicative voice ("This has been done"). In the cross, the all-encompassing love of God speaks louder than the accusing voice of God's law.[11] Our guilt has been atoned for and the deepest judgment satisfied, opening up the reconciliation of sinners with a holy God and life eternal.

Furthermore, while the law is conditional—a two-way street—the gospel is unconditional. Like all true gifts, God's grace comes with no strings attached, an incongruous and superabundant surprise to all who receive it. The underlying logic of grace is the inverse of the law: love and blessing are bestowed on needy creatures like you and me, independent of merit and before any demonstration of value. God actively seeks out the lost and the broken and the sinful so that he might redeem them. Christian hope, therefore, lies not in having to generate goodness or love on our own steam but in prior belovedness, expressed in sacrificial terms and despite our not deserving it.

In a life governed by the law, the fear of defeat and threat of scarcity loom over every endeavor. We must tediously craft text messages with just the right balance of assertiveness and deference. In the realm of the gospel, we can risk being vulnerable, without fear of what trouble or embarrassment our words might bring.

It goes without saying that many iterations of Christianity, as well as of other religions, stress obedience to the law over the freedom of grace. Secular "replacement religions" mimic this pattern, albeit with lower stakes. If you eat well enough, vote well enough, parent well enough, you will *be* enough. But any form of religion that is primarily concerned with achieving righteousness through the law will be preoccupied with coloring within the lines. These versions of the faith are not known for their joy. Few things are more drab (or constrictive) than the self-consciousness and endless pulse-taking of a life under the lens of scrupulous obedience.

11. You might say that if the law commands that we love perfectly, the gospel proclaims that we are perfectly loved.

There is no use being indirect here: such a view represents a tragic and destructive misunderstanding of the Christian gospel, as well as a misreading of Scripture. In 2 Corinthians 3:17, Paul writes that "the Lord is the Spirit, and where the Spirit of the Lord is, there is freedom." This freedom is understood elsewhere to exist in contrast to the spirit of slavery that applies to those "under the law," a slavery from which Christ has set believers free. This is a large part of what Paul meant when he penned his great proclamation, perhaps the fever pitch of his letter to the Romans: "Therefore there is now no condemnation for those who are in Christ Jesus. For the law of the Spirit of life in Christ Jesus has set you free from the law of sin and of death" (8:1–2).

Freedom from the law is not theoretical or abstract. If the law has been, in a very real sense, *deactivated* for those who are in Christ, then the condemnation that the law levels at limited and sinful creatures such as ourselves loses its bite. We are freed from fear of not just punishment but also judgment. And this freedom *from* carries a freedom *to* in its wings.

In the wake of the Big Relief, the key question of life becomes one of freedom: What would you do, what risk would you take, what would you say, if you weren't afraid? If you weren't afraid of letting anyone down, or missing out on some future opportunity, or of some catastrophe befalling you if you let go of your grip on things? That is to say, what would you do if all threat was removed, and you didn't *have* to do anything? What would you do if you could undertake something for the sheer joy of doing it, rather than any outcome it might produce?

The Opposite of Dance Lessons

The answer to these questions, I'm convinced, looks a lot like a grandfather and his two grandsons doing cannonballs off beaten-up desks into a swimming pool. I'm referring to a scene in the movie *The Royal Tenenbaums*, directed by Wes Anderson. The titular character, played by Gene Hackman, spends the film attempting to endear himself to the eccentric family he walked out on decades before. His oldest son, Chaz, is a widower with two young boys of his own. After observing how tight of a regimen the grieving Chaz keeps his boys on, Royal comments to his ex-wife, Ethel, "You can't raise boys to be scared of life. You got to brew some recklessness into them." She says that's terrible advice, but he knows she doesn't really think so.

In the next scene, Royal asks his grandsons what they do for fun. When they mention the self-defense classes that their father signed them up for, Royal cuts them off: "I'm not talking about dance lessons. I'm talking about putting a brick through the other guy's windshield. I'm talking about taking it out and chopping it up."

We then watch a giddy montage of the boys and their granddad riding go-karts through a construction zone, throwing water balloons at a passing taxi, hitching unauthorized rides on the back of a garbage truck. There's joy on their faces as they get a taste of freedom from the treadmill of productivity and protectiveness to which their father has, in his grief, chained them. Their grandfather grants them the occasion to play, and they receive it as grace—which is to say, respite from the law of getting things done (and keeping bad at bay).[12]

Play is the key word here. Like resonance, it is one of those know-it-when-you-see-it experiences in life. Sometimes an activity can feel like play in one context but not another. Making a sandcastle on the beach with toddlers is play. Making a sand sculpture with other adults to enter a competition is not quite the same thing. A pickup game of touch football is play; an NFL playoff game, with millions of dollars on the line, less so. Impromptu kitchen karaoke is play, a vocal recital not so much.

At root, play is not a means to an end but an end in itself. Something can be understood and experienced as play when it's undertaken for its own sake, rather than to get something else. The moment you

12. *The Royal Tenenbaums*, directed by Wes Anderson (Touchstone Pictures, 2001).

are doing something to aid in accomplishing some future goal, you are no longer at play. Many of us, myself included, play pickleball because we genuinely enjoy the sport—especially those satisfyingly loud pops—not because it yields any reward.

Play, in other words, is noninstrumental. This is why we understand it to be the opposite of work. Work has an end in mind, whether that be earning a wage or producing a product (to sell). Play is something we do simply because we like doing it. It *may* produce a result, but that's not why we do it. In fact, play is foreign to results-oriented thinking, which tends to trap us in a hoped-for future. Play, like resonance, roots a person in the present. In this sense, everyone plays, not just toddlers or dogs or middle school boys. Think of the student who studies hard because they are fascinated by the material as opposed to the student who studies hard to earn the best grade (which will advance them somehow). The former has cultivated an attitude toward their studies that we might call playful.

In addition, and following directly from this open-endedness, play is an expression of freedom. If you undertake a given activity out of fear or coercion, it will not be play. Play is intrinsically motivated. When an activity is unhooked from threat and pressure, it becomes play. Remember, no one gets graded at recess. Sure, there may be winners and losers in a game, but it won't be truly play unless the stakes are benign. As theorist Brian Sutton-Smith observes, "All forms of play promise that one can never quite lose while still at play."[13] Indeed, play is motivated by delight, not judgment. To return to pickleball, I suspect that part of the game's explosion in popularity has to do with the fact that no one grew up playing it competitively. We are therefore free from comparison with our past selves. It also feels faintly ridiculous, which is part of the fun. Play, for this reason, is almost always dynamic, a place to experiment, take risks, and safely fail.[14]

13. Brian Sutton-Smith, *The Ambiguity of Play* (Harvard University Press, 1997), 212.
14. No one illustrates this aspect of play more memorably than Bill Watterson in his strip *Calvin and Hobbes*, specifically in the game of Calvinball.

We might accentuate other aspects of play. Play tends to be relational, for instance. It also tends to be creative and transportive, like a trip to an alternate universe where alternate rules apply—or no rules at all. Spike a ball at someone on the street and you will be reproved at best. Do it on a volleyball court, and you'll be cheered.

Play is good for us.[15] More than a few experts have linked the decline in free play among children to inversely high rates of anxiety, depression, and suicide among young people.[16]

And play is closely bound up in the experience of God's grace. Nigerian theologian Nimi Wariboko connects the dots for us when he writes that "the logic of grace is the logic of play." He says,

> Grace . . . by definition is a genuine gift and not a secretly instrumentalized one. Freely it is given and freely it is received. It has no purpose. No self-addressed envelope from the giver to send something in return. . . . It is a pure means of relations between the believer and God. It is play, not because it is trivial and worthless, but because it has no end, an unended action. . . . It is the state of religion that is deprived of the spur of necessity, want, and purpose—human-divine relationship reorganized in the spirit of play.[17]

The spirit of play is not so much a type of behavior as an attitude undergirding life in the shadow of the Big Relief. Those steeped in

---

15. It is so good for us, in fact, that we can, in our accelerating haste, attempt to instrumentalize it. Heather Havrilesky warns us about the potential subversion of play in an aptly titled article for *The Baffler*: "Play, Dammit!" She writes,
> The vigorous exhortation to "play" now haunts every corner of our culture. Typically issued as an imperative along with words like *breathe* and *meditate* and *dance* and *celebrate*, the word *play* . . . has a curious way of repelling the senses, conjuring as it does all manner of mandatory frivolity. . . . Yet Johan Huizinga, the Dutch cultural theorist who tirelessly examined "the play element in culture," asserted that the one defining feature of play is that it's voluntary. "Play to order is no longer play," he declared flatly. (Heather Havrilesky, "Play, Dammit!," *The Baffler*, January 2014, https://thebaffler.com/salvos/play-dammit, emphasis in original)

16. Jonathan Haidt, *The Anxious Generation: How the Great Rewiring of Childhood Is Causing an Epidemic of Mental Illness* (Penguin Random House, 2024), 23–31, 51–53.

17. Nimi Wariboko, *The Pentecostal Principle: Ethical Methodology in New Spirit* (Eerdmans, 2012), 183–84.

the Bible might call it living by the Spirit. This attitude syncs with the one that Jesus himself summons in Matthew 18:2–3: "[Jesus] called a child, whom he put among them, and said, 'Truly I tell you, unless you change and become like children, you will never enter the kingdom of heaven.'" The only thing children do is play. At least, that's what they do after their immediate needs are provided for—and before acceleration gets hold of them.

In his article "Defining and Recognizing Play," biologist Gordon Burghardt observes that animals play more often when they are "adequately fed, clothed, healthy, and not under stress." He calls this state a "relaxed field," a setting in which threats have been removed, or at least are not perceived.[18] Commenting on Burghardt's work, my brother Simeon Zahl writes, "Life in the Spirit, under the grace of God, is the ultimate relaxed field. Resting in the relaxed field generated by the reality of divine grace, the Christian, like the securely attached child, is liberated to experiment, to explore, and to get it wrong."[19]

The Big Relief announces that the high-wire game of proving ourselves is finished. By grace, the lingering threat of judgment has been removed. By grace, all that remains is unended action. This is less an invitation to a do-nothing existence of insipid frivolity than an invitation to creative and joyful risk-taking.

If Jesus's righteousness is truly yours, then your worth is no longer indexed to your productivity. You do not have to achieve perfection. You don't have to beat last year's results. You don't have to optimize your extracurriculars. In fact, you don't have to focus on yourself at all. Not when there's fun to be had and socks to be snagged. Just be sure to clear the room before you start playing. Oh, and pro-tip: there's no rule against donning multiple pairs.

18. Gordon M. Burghardt, "Defining and Recognizing Play," in *The Oxford Handbook of the Development of Play*, ed. Anthony D. Pellegrini (Oxford University Press, 2010): 16, https://doi.org/10.1093/oxfordhb/9780195393002.013.0002.

19. Simeon Zahl, "Play and Freedom: Patterns of Life in the Spirit," *International Journal of Systematic Theology* 26, no. 2 (April 2024): 212–15, https://doi.org/10.1111/ijst.12661.

9

Rescue

The Relief from Captivity (and Death)

We couldn't hold out any longer. We had kept the peer pressure at bay for years. We had listened to the pleas, heard the arguments, and absorbed the tantrums. We had held our ground as best we could. But this next Christmas would mark the end. The fight was over, and my wife and I were giving in.

It was time for our oldest son to get his first smartphone.

Surely some parents don't agonize over this decision, but I have yet to meet them. The subject inspires defensiveness and guilt pretty much across the board. We've lived with this technology long enough to know what it does to adolescents, let alone the rest of us.[1] A friend

1. For example, when the Center for Disease Control and Prevention released its bi-annual Youth Risk Behavior Survey in 2023, they reported that a *majority* of teenage girls in the United States (57 percent) now say that they experience persistent sadness or hopelessness (up from 36 percent in 2011). Thirty percent of that same group now report having seriously considered suicide (up from 19 percent in 2011). The increases for boys were less dramatic, though still significant. While smartphone usage isn't the only factor here—see chap. 8 on the decline in free play—there is increasing evidence that the devices have contributed substantially to the adolescent mental health crisis, particularly in how they provide access to social media platforms. For detailed data and analysis, see Jean M. Twenge, *Generations: The Real Differences Between Gen Z, Millennials, Gen X, Boomers, and Silents—and What They Mean for America's Future* (Atria Books, 2023).

141

of mine said he'd buy his fourteen-year-old a keg of beer before he'd get him an iPhone.

What was our tipping point, you ask? We didn't mind him being out of touch when he biked around the neighborhood or shot baskets at the park, nor did we really care about not being able to reach him if we were running late for a pickup. He could wait around, just like we had as kids. Boredom builds character (or so they say). We weren't even that concerned about the content he'd have access to, as most of these devices have robust parental filters.

The straw that broke the parents' back was the dawning realization that the social life of our son's age group was happening almost exclusively via group text messages. By not allowing him a phone my wife and I were making it more difficult for our son to make friends. We had just moved him to a new school where he was—by his report, mind you—the last kid in his grade without one. We felt strongly that it was our duty, as journalist Kathryn Jezer-Morton puts it, to "prolong the time in [our] kids' lives when they aren't on standing reserve for their device."[2] But it's heart-wrenching to imagine your child eating his lunch alone—especially when you know you could do something about it. And so Santa got the memo. Our son would join us in captivity.

I took consolation from the fact that phones aren't the only things that take us captive. Maybe growing up has more to do with figuring out which sort of captivity we can stomach than with avoiding it altogether. Fear can hold us captive, as can depression, embarrassment, and self-recrimination. Poverty can hold a person captive, and so can inherited wealth. Trauma often holds a person captive. I often feel like I'm captive to my body, its need for sleep and trans fats. As for our son, I suppose we got to the point where we were willing to trade captivity to ostracization for captivity to the algorithm. But perhaps I'm just rationalizing a jellified backbone.

2. Kathryn Jezer-Morton, "Why Does Giving My Son His First Phone Feel Like a Trap?," *Cut*, September 19, 2022, https://www.thecut.com/2022/09/giving-my-son-his-first-phone-feels-like-a-trap.html.

Captivity is a strong and provocative word. It connotes being held against one's will, imprisoned and disempowered, no longer chief over one's own life. These are neither flattering nor fashionable associations. We much prefer to think of ourselves as captains of our own ships, masters of our own fates, or—vomiting emoji—CEOs of our own personal brands. Sadly, the reality of life in a worn-out world usually veers closer to the experience of addiction.

When an alcoholic admits, in the first of the twelve steps, that they are powerless over alcohol, they are admitting their captivity to the substance. They are confessing that the lock to their particular cell cannot be opened from the inside but requires outside help, in the form of a higher power.

Still, we make a grave mistake if we limit the scope of addiction to substances. I often wonder if there are as many addictions as there are people. If you're addicted to approval, then you are captive to what others think of you and thus will do anything you can to attain and maintain that approval. If you're addicted to self-pity, you will find yourself compulsively spinning every situation into a woe-is-me victim narrative. It can be highly intoxicating. It could be that, like me, sugar has you shackled. Perhaps your addiction is socially acceptable. You used to be addicted to painkillers but then got clean, and now you're addicted to showing the world you're a success story. It could be that you're one of those insufferable souls who's addicted to the endorphins that come from working out—in which case, I hope you know how lucky you are (and how much some of us resent you). Work is another addiction that we tend to approve of as a society. Ask the child of a workaholic about their experience of their parent, though, and I guarantee the condition will be cast in a less pleasing light.

Captives Anonymous

This isn't a flattering picture of humanity, but it goes a lot further in explaining our strange and often self-defeating behavior than the ship-captain model. Why does my sister keep getting back together with that guy who treats her so terribly? Why do I scroll through my news feed whenever I feel anxious, when scrolling only ever makes the anxiety worse? Why do I keep criticizing my spouse when that has never produced the slightest change in behavior and only seems to alienate us further? You stand a much better chance of loving other people when you see them as fellow captives, as opposed to, say, yelling at them to free themselves.[3]

The great question is not *if* we are captives but *how* we approach our captivity. Plenty of us, it must be said, make peace with our captivity. We are happy prisoners, for a while. We learn to manage our disordered eating—until the day it becomes unmanageable. The alcoholic can see glimpses of their problematic state but is usually able to adopt the chaos as normal. The same goes for codependency. Our captivity can get awfully comfortable, save for a dramatic loss that cuts through the denial.

More commonly, we cycle through fixes. We move houses, and the family gets along better for a stretch. We meet someone new and think, "Finally, this is the relationship I won't sabotage." A financial investment pays off, and the windfall makes us feel secure and good about ourselves—for a couple weeks. None of these things are bad in and of themselves. It is only when we lean on them as self-salvation projects that the seams start showing. Alas, there's a big difference between rearranging the furniture within our prison cell and actually getting out. Pastor Nadia Bolz-Weber refers to these sorts of fixes when she confesses, "For most of my life I have relied pretty heavily on me-based solutions to all my me-based problems. Even when my solutions don't work, at least they are mine."[4] Bolz-Weber is articulating the pressure we feel to fix and even save ourselves—and, as with the other pressures we've cataloged, it is not absent from the church.

3. I explore these dynamics at considerable length in *Low Anthropology: The Unlikely Key to a Gracious View of Others (and Yourself)* (Brazos, 2022).
4. Nadia Bolz-Weber, "Notes from a Late Bloomer," *Corners* (blog), February 26, 2024, https://thecorners.substack.com/p/notes-from-a-late-bloomer.

I'd go so far as to say that a great deal of what passes for Christian living is some form of self-salvation that's been given a religious gloss. We believe that if we pray fervently, attend church faithfully, give sacrificially, or understand the right theology deeply enough, our problems will go away. We will avoid pain. It is seldom said outright, but such a posture quickly becomes a form of trusting in our own abilities and behaviors rather than in the work of the Holy Spirit. We look to the law rather than grace to deliver us from captivity, to spiritual technique rather than faith. Soon our shackles are as heavy as they've ever been; they just have crosses emblazoned on them now.

And yet there are worse types of shackles to wear, if for no other reason than the meaning of the cross cannot be obscured indefinitely. This central Christian symbol speaks louder than any attempt to domesticate it—both the extent of human captivity and the lengths to which God is willing to go to break those chains. That is, our captivity runs so deep that somehow our liberation needed the death of Jesus. We are captive to the behaviors and addictions mentioned earlier only because in a more universal sense, you and I are captive to sin and—dare I say it—the powers of darkness.

I See a Darkness

Sin is a tricky word. It has to less to do with individual misdeeds and more to do with disordered desire. It names the way we love the wrong things too much and the right things too little, such that our best plans go askew and we frequently hurt the ones we love. It's almost as though we live with an internal distortion field that is constantly twisting our affections in a self-seeking direction. Sin is the inherited condition of fallen humanity—the internal dimension of our captivity—and not something we can escape through exertion or conceptualization.

The phrase *powers of darkness*, however, refers to the observable reality that malign factors exist beyond us, such that we often feel we are under assault and even overpowered by forces outside our control. These forces do not have our best interests at heart. It used to be more difficult to talk about such things in polite society. Serious people did not entertain nonmaterialistic accounts of the world, at least not outwardly. I'm not sure what happened to soften that stridency—why, for example, radical atheism fell out of fashion so swiftly or Silicon Valley went woo.[5] Perhaps wellness culture hit the internet at the precise moment that a generation raised on Harry Potter came of age. Maybe the heady narratives of scientific and political progress just rang too hollow amid the vicious tribalism of contemporary culture wars. For whatever reason, the mention of "bad vibes" or "negative energy" no longer draws the same degree of suspicion it did in decades past.

I suspect, however, that this renewed openness to—or non-embarrassment about—invisible malefactors mainly has to do with the vocabulary of systemic oppression. When we speak of an institution being infected by racism or misogyny, it often sounds like there's a disembodied spirit holding that structure captive. Maybe there is! The Bible claims that there is such a thing as evil and that it has intention and power. This is a frightening truth to acknowledge, but as a lifetime of horror movies has taught me, not every bad thing reduces to brain chemistry or trauma. Jesus didn't just forgive sins; he also exorcised demons. We might call this the external component of human captivity.

The cross announces that God cares about human captivity so much that he is willing to die to set us free. He will not leave us imprisoned. This facet does not come out of nowhere: Jesus's concern for captives was there from the start. Early in the Gospel of Luke, just as his years of public ministry are beginning, Jesus visits his

5. *Woo* is a contemporary colloquialism for what people in the nineties used to call *New Age*. It refers to heterodox spiritual practices and beliefs that border on the occult yet usually fall more into the realm of "kooky." Tara Isabella Burton gives a probing account of how such attitudes have risen in popularity among American technocrats in her essay "Rational Magic: Why a Silicon Valley Culture That Was Once Obsessed with Reason Is Going Woo," *New Atlantis*, no. 72 (Spring 2023), https://www.thenewatlantis.com/publications/rational-magic.

hometown of Nazareth. He enters a synagogue on the Sabbath and reads aloud from the scroll of Isaiah, a portion of the sixty-first chapter:

> The Spirit of the Lord is upon me,
>   because he has anointed me
>   to bring good news to the poor.
> He has sent me to proclaim release to the captives
>   and recovery of sight to the blind,
>   to set free those who are oppressed,
>   to proclaim the year of the Lord's favor. (Luke 4:18–19)

Jesus then hands the scroll back to the attendant, sits down, and says, "Today this scripture has been fulfilled in your hearing" (4:21). It is one of the great mic drops in the New Testament.

What's so amazing about this episode is that it shows that Jesus understood his purpose as having to do with captives. He came to proclaim their release. Other versions of the Bible translate "release" as "liberty" or "deliverance."

Thankfully, his conception of captivity was broad. He did not, for example, walk from the synagogue directly to the local jail (or Roman garrison) to break out those who were incarcerated there. No doubt he cared about criminals—the thief on the cross being just one example (Luke 23:43)—but Jesus's initial acts of deliverance targeted people who were captive to illness and infirmity and possession (and the resulting degradation and shame).

Jesus is not just a teacher or healer; he is a savior. He comes to rescue captives—that is, real people with intractable problems—from the prisons they live in, both the prisons we make for ourselves and the ones the world makes for us. When I think of what salvation from captivity looks like in practice, I recall a scene in the Johnny Cash biopic, *Walk the Line*, where Johnny is detoxing from painkillers, completely delirious after crashing his tractor. We hear the roar of an engine, and the camera pans to the driveway outside the house, where Johnny's drug dealer has just pulled up. He is there to supply Johnny with more of what's torturing him. Out walks Johnny's long-suffering wife, June Carter, with a shotgun in her hand. She doesn't say anything because she doesn't need to. Her eyes are shouting, "Get thee behind me, Satan!" She stands against the forces of darkness—within and without—and saves Johnny.[6]

There is one more point we shouldn't miss from the passage that Jesus reads aloud in the synagogue. Yes, Jesus is the liberator. But it is the Holy Spirit that is the engine of our liberation: "The Spirit of the Lord is upon me" is the line from Isaiah that he reads first.

The great privilege of attending the same church for years is not only that you get to hear about the Big Relief every week but also that you get to witness the work of the Spirit in a person's life. When my friend Greg showed up at a service ten years ago—by accident—he was a physical and emotional wreck. Life had not been kind. He wouldn't look you in the eye when you spoke to him. I remember he almost had a panic attack the first time he came up for Communion. My colleagues and I were honestly afraid he would faint. But he kept coming back, drinking in the Big Relief as though he couldn't get enough. Ten years later, just before going off to seminary, the guy was reading lessons aloud to the congregation every week and running outreach trips to Nicaragua, his demeanor completely altered.

I think of another attendee who washed up on the banks of our church about twelve years ago, deeply demoralized from a nasty divorce. She radiated bitterness and prickliness. Today, when we have someone dealing with a marital breakdown, her number is the one I give out. She'd be the first to tell you that, despite coming from a buttoned-up background that had little time for Jesus (or anything that welcomed weakness), the Spirit liberated her from her resentments, and now all she wants to do is be of service. Of course, take a trip to our church basement, and the stories of recovery you'll hear from the attendees of the Alcoholics and Narcotics Anonymous

6. *Walk the Line*, directed by James Mangold (Fox 2000 Productions, 2005).

groups that meet there will spin your head around. Whenever we talk about how God has done for us what we could not do for ourselves, we are talking about the work of the Holy Spirit.

Liberations like these don't happen according to a predictable timeline. Sometimes they don't happen at all. They almost always take a different form than you'd expect. But at this point, I've seen far too many people released from far too many captivities to deny the Spirit's presence in the world.

The Final Captivity

Okay, okay. Perhaps you see how this form of rescue would appeal to addicts and social pariahs and canceled celebrities. But what about us law-abiding citizens who are basically doing all right in life? Everyone has problems, and some of those problems have a compulsive element, but using the word *captive* seems a bridge too far—and possibly shame-inducing. "My people-pleasing may be a drag, but it's more of a psychological quirk that I'm working on with my therapist than an addiction that I need intervention for." I hope that's true, and for some folks it no doubt is. I do not wish to intimate that we are captive in every aspect of our lives. With help, people overcome besetting patterns of dysfunction and sin all the time.

Yet even among the victorious strivers out there, I'd wager there is at least one area where the language of captivity applies, one place in our lives where we yearn not for resources but for rescue. If that place hasn't made itself known yet, it will. I say that with confidence and without any intended condescension. It doesn't matter who we are or how impressive our capabilities, we are alike in one core respect: our mortality. Modern medicine and the science of longevity may give us a few extra years with our loved ones, and mindfulness may grant us a modicum of serenity, but none of these things can postpone the end indefinitely. Each and every one of us will die. You and I may balk at thinking of ourselves as in need of rescue in other instances, but not here. Here the truth of our predicament crystallizes: we are all Goonies.

Hear me out.

As a child of the 1980s, my imagination was shaped in large part by the films produced by Amblin Entertainment, the company formed by Steven Spielberg, Kathleen Kennedy, and Frank Marshall. We have Amblin to thank for *E.T. the Extra-Terrestrial*, *Gremlins*, and *Back to the Future*, not to mention the vastly underrated *Young Sherlock Holmes*. These movies combined adventure, humor, fantasy, and coming of age with expert storytelling in a way that didn't talk down to kids.[7] No Amblin project did this better than *The Goonies* (1985).

The Goonies follows a group of prepubescent outcasts as they search for lost treasure in their hometown of Astoria, Oregon. They are after the fabled trove of the pirate One-Eyed Willie, which they believe will save their houses from being demolished by real estate developers. Their quest takes an urgent turn when they run into the nefarious family of counterfeiters, the Fratellis, on the lam from the police. The Fratellis catch wind of what the kids are hunting and follow them into heavily booby-trapped tunnels that lead to the gold. The film climaxes with a confrontation on Willie's legendary ship, which the Goonies discover hidden in a cave off the coast. A century beforehand, the pirates had evidently blocked the entrance with enormous boulders and rigged the place with explosives that would cause it to collapse if anyone tried to make off with their booty.

Needless to say, that's exactly what happens. After the showdown triggers a cave-in, we watch as the kids scramble to find a way out. They find none. That is, not until Amblin's most memorable Christ figure, Sloth, steps in. Sloth is a Fratelli sibling but not a proud one. The nature of his physical deformities is never explained, nor his apparent mental limitations, which make speaking difficult. What is clear, however, is that Sloth has been terribly abused by his family of origin, who had chained him up in the basement of their hideout to

---

7. Amblin continues to inspire intense waves of nostalgia today, the *Stranger Things* television series being the most well-known example.

contain his mammoth physical strength. When the Goonies appear on the scene, Sloth befriends young Chunk.

The kids have nowhere left to run. Their villainous pursuers have caught up to them. The boulders now blocking the exit are too heavy, and time is running out. They are completely stuck and cannot save themselves. Enter Sloth, who intervenes by—slowly, painfully— lifting a giant boulder on his back. Light streams in. The kids crawl through his legs to safety and freedom. Where there was no way out, Sloth makes a way, sacrificing his body to rescue his weaker friends from certain death.[8]

I reach for this image not to trivialize the rescue of God but because it is so vivid—and lodged so deeply in my own imagination (and that of my generation). When we find ourselves boxed in by life and all roads appear to be blocked—when our efforts to engineer our own salvation have failed and the sky is falling—Jesus offers a way through. Not *one* way among many but *a* way where there appears to be none.

Rescue from sin and death—this is undoubtedly the biggest aspect of the Big Relief. In Romans, Paul makes this connection explicit: "Death no longer has dominion over [Christ]. The death he died, he died to sin once for all, but the life he lives, he lives to God. So you also must consider yourselves dead to sin and alive to God in Christ Jesus. . . . For sin will have no dominion over you, since you are not under law but under grace" (6:9–11, 14).

In other words, Jesus does not give his disciples a set of rules to follow. He doesn't draw captives a new and improved layout for their prison cells, nor does he introduce a fresh technique for picking locks. Jesus does not *show* the way; he *is* the way. As author Francis Spufford so beautifully puts it, Jesus is "the shining your shame cannot extinguish." He is "the door where you thought there was only a wall."[9]

8. *The Goonies*, directed by Richard Donner (Amblin Entertainment, 1985).
9. Francis Spufford, *Unapologetic: Why, Despite Everything, Christianity Can Still Make Surprising Emotional Sense* (HarperCollins, 2013), 142.

What, we might reasonably ask, does this door open? Phrased another way, what does Jesus rescue us from and what does he rescue us for? I'm not talking about the here and now, as beautiful and important as that dimension may be. I'm talking about what may be the tightest of all theological corners: the afterlife. In doing so, I realize I'm broaching a subject that by definition is both speculative and otherworldly. Usually, the less said the better, so I'll say it as plain as I can.

I've always understood that Jesus rescues God's wayward children from alienation from the Father. Another word for this alienation is *hell*.[10] This is where captivity to sin and self leads spiritually, just as it leads there relationally. Separation from the source of all life—that is, God—is synonymous with *annihilation* at best. But there I go already, making cosmological leaps that I don't really understand and are impossible to back up. All I know is that Jesus seemed to operate on the assumption that eternal stakes are at play for souls such as ours. He was never capricious, though, and was reliably gracious. That second part cannot be overstated.

As for what Jesus rescues us for, I take the old-fashioned view that when we die, our souls go to be with God. What exactly that means, who can say? I tend to concur with what author Marilynne Robinson said when asked if she thought about heaven more as she got older: "I belong to a particular branch of Protestantism that sort of discourages reflections on heaven in the sense that we can't know what it is and we can't know on what grounds we might or might not end up there. I find that very satisfying. . . . When I die, I expect to be very impressed with what follows."[11]

Thankfully, the Bible does gives us a few pictures of kingdom come to go on. The one that resounds with the most relief in my ears

10. Unfortunately, I can't read that word without Gary Larson's *The Far Side* cartoon immediately popping into my brain. For a sampling, visit https://screenrant.com/10-funniest-far-side-comics-set-in-hell/.

11. David Marchese, "Marilynne Robinson Considers Biden a Gift of God," *New York Times*, February 23, 2024, https://www.nytimes.com/interactive/2024/02/18/magazine/marilynne-robinson-interview.html.

is the promise that, when all the stones in front of all the caves are rolled away, "[God] will wipe every tear from their eyes. Death will be no more; mourning and crying and pain will be no more, for the first things have passed away" (Rev. 21:4). Has a more magnificent promise ever been made?

One day we are all going to need rescuing from the abyss. One day the dark will be closing in for good. When that happens, what blessed relief it will be to find Jesus in the dark there with us, arms open and ready to pull us out into the new light, whatever that might be! I wouldn't want to restrict the glory to what I'm capable of imagining.

For now, though, I suppose all we can do is return in faith to terra firma and the simple proclamation that God gives life to those who have every reason to expect death. Jesus mediates, Jesus ransoms, Jesus rescues, and yes, Jesus saves—a lot like English recreational cave diver Rick Stanton.

Another Cave, Another Diver

Perhaps you remember the news story of the Thai youth soccer team that got stranded deep underground in 2018. I remembered it in the same way I remembered the dramatic rescue effort to save a child who fell down a well in a town near where we lived when I was in elementary school: as an uplifting headline that testified to the strength of the human spirit. It wasn't until watching the Academy Award–winning documentary *The Rescue* (2021) that I got a sense of the (much) stranger-than-fiction miracle that occurred in the Tham Luang Nang Non cave system.

What follows is a snapshot. On June 23, 2018, twelve junior soccer players, ages eleven to sixteen, and their assistant coach went exploring a local cave after practice. While they were inside, it started to rain. Before they realized what was happening, the sky was dropping buckets, and the way out of the cave flooded, trapping them inside. Their only way to avoid drowning was to head farther into the caves.

When the boys did not return home that evening, parents alerted the head coach, who traced their movements to the cave's entrance. All the boys' bikes and belongings were still there, so he alerted the authorities. The rain continued to pour, and by the time the Royal Thai Navy SEALs arrived on the scene, things were looking dire. The water was so murky that even with high-intensity lights, the SEALs couldn't see anything.

Through an unlikely series of events, a local diver put the SEALs in contact with the British Cave Rescue Council, a group of recreational cave divers from halfway around the world. Two volunteers, Rick Stanton and John Volanthen, hopped on the first plane they could and joined in the search. It is worth noting here that cave diving, like free diving, is not your run-of-the-mill hobby. Spending weekends underwater in a pitch-black cave in a remote part of the British Midlands does not appeal to most people. It requires bespoke gear, extensive training, and, at least in Stanton's case, a penchant for otherworldly solitude. These are eccentric guys, in other words, a far cry from the tanned Hollywood superstars or pro-athletes we usually associate with acts of heroism. When God gets involved, things often get a little weird.

After they arrived, Stanton and Volanthen were joined by armed forces from the United States and Australia. With each passing day, as the media began to run with the story, the rain kept falling, preventing the men from searching the caves adequately. At 10:00 p.m. on July 2, ten days after they'd gone missing, Stanton and Volanthen finally came upon the boys, all of whom were somehow still alive, held captive by the water two and a half miles from the cave mouth.

There was no pretense that these boys could save themselves. They needed much more than a helping hand or a detailed map to the surface. Awareness of their shared predicament may have bonded them together and softened those days spent in the dark. But solidarity wouldn't save them. It was either rescue or death. So it is with us. The recognition of our shared captivity can go a long way toward evoking compassion and warmth, but ultimately some form of intervention will have to occur if lasting hope is to be gained.

Then came the impossible part. In order to extract the boys safely, the divers would have to sedate each child and drag them, one by one, on their backs through four kilometers of barely translucent water. The journey out would take about three hours per child, but because the anesthetic would wear off after forty-five minutes, the divers would have to stop multiple times to readminister. The divers also had to take care to keep their heads higher than the boys so that, when things got especially tight, the divers would hit their own heads against the rocks first. Calling the rescue attempt precarious would be supremely optimistic. It was going to take a miracle.

And yet, that is what happened. Death was defied, yet in a way that looked like it was being embraced. Every single boy made it out alive, stunning the onlookers, the organizers, and the media. No one had dared expect a 100 percent survival rate.[12] The Big Relief came as a big surprise.

Once all the boys were safe, the parents held a ceremony to give thanks to the peculiar Englishmen. In the documentary, one of them looks at the stoic Stanton and says, "On behalf of all the parents I want to thank you. It's like our children have died and been given another life."[13] I couldn't believe my ears or eyes. These boys had been released from captivity by a gang of the most unlikely saviors imaginable. The soccer players were completely passive during their salvation, unconscious in fact. They weren't consulted about the extraction plan. They hadn't even asked anyone to come looking for them. They couldn't! All they contributed was their lostness. You couldn't script a more uncanny illustration of Christian salvation. In fact, had *The Rescue* been scripted, I doubt anyone would've produced it. Not even Amblin. Simply too far-fetched.

12. On July 5, a Royal Thai SEAL named Saman Kunan drowned while bringing three oxygen tanks to the rescue divers.

13. *The Rescue*, directed by Jimmy Chin and Elizabeth Chai Vasarhelyi (National Geographic Documentary Films, 2021).

Life instead of certain death: this is the Biggest Relief imaginable. Because of God's grace, it is not up to you to free yourself from captivity, nor is it up to your spouse or your child or your pastor. Rescuer is *God's* job description.

Maybe *job* is the wrong word though, because God is not obliged to rescue anyone. Rescue isn't his burden but his delight—the sort of thing he'd do on weekends if the opportunity arose. God doesn't have to save; he loves to save. An eccentric to the end, this God of grace.

CONCLUSION

Love and Mercy

I can pinpoint the moment that grace took hold of my heart. I remember where I was, what I was doing, and what prompted it.

I'm not talking about a religious conversion. That was several years away at the time (and remains a work in progress). And I'm not talking about an intellectual epiphany. I still don't fully understand the Big Relief and don't think I ever will, thank God. But something happened one day to plant the seed of this book, if not the rest of my life.

The year was 1995, and I was about to start my junior year of high school.[1] The previous semester I'd stumbled on something special at my school library: a brand new five-CD box set of music by The Beach Boys. I had enjoyed their songs as a kid but largely stopped listening once teenage angst (a.k.a. Nirvana) set in. The box piqued my interest though. More than half the material had never been released on CD. Unless you had a turntable—which no one did at that point—this stuff had been lost.

The tracks veered from the sublime to the cringeworthy to the avant-garde, sometimes in the same recording. Other than the uniformly angelic voices, it bore little resemblance to the surfer tunes

1. I was just about to head off to water polo preseason training, in fact.

that had grabbed me in elementary school. I was mesmerized. The box took up residence in my room that spring, a pocket universe for me to visit whenever I needed escape or comfort.

Cut to the summer and the news that head beach boy Brian Wilson was emerging from a long hibernation. The 1980s, like the 1970s, had not been kind to Wilson. This was pre-internet, so all that fans had to go on were rumors that a domineering therapist had taken control of Wilson—body, soul, and bank account. It was ugly and alarming but also reportedly in the past. The legendary composer was ready to reengage and had been coaxed back into the studio to record new versions of his old songs. The sessions were filmed in black and white and released as the documentary *I Just Wasn't Made for These Times*.

As soon as I heard about it, I tracked down a copy at our local video rental store and pressed play. During interviews, Wilson didn't look at the camera, and when he spoke, it was out of one side of his mouth in slurred sentences that weren't entirely cogent. He seemed profoundly uncomfortable. The man's struggles with mental illness and recreational drugs were well known—he spent fifteen years in bed at one point—but it was still a shock to see how much life had ravaged him.

Then it happened. In the closing stretch of the movie, someone brings up the "weird scene" that Wilson endured in the '80s with the exploitative therapist. The camera cuts to Wilson, sitting at a piano looking forlorn. He says, "I remember my assistant from the '80s, who never left me alone. I said I gotta dump my feelings on the keyboard. My chest feels so bad. My soul aches so much. And I just went in there and went . . ." He plays a descending chord progression, and then, in that melancholy tenor of his, sings, "Love and mercy, that's what you need tonight."[2]

The song, which I'd never heard before, was simple yet gorgeous, full of both pathos and hope, and it was flowing out of the mouth

---

2. *I Just Wasn't Made for These Times*, directed by Don Was (Cro Magnon Productions, 1995).

of a severely damaged vessel. "A lotta people out there hurtin' and it really scares me," goes the second verse before Wilson repeats his prayer for love and mercy.[3] The answer to suffering, both his own and the world's, was clear. It wasn't vengeance or punishment, technique or knowledge, but that precious combination of love and mercy known as grace. Other singers might say the same words, but hearing the message from someone who had suffered so much—and was suffering still—I couldn't help in that moment *believing* it.

It wasn't just the content of the song that resonated. I felt like I was glimpsing an underlayer of reality, something truer than true. Here, as elsewhere, Wilson's gift was so superabundant yet so jarringly out of proportion—incongruous!—to the man himself. What was pouring out of him wasn't the result of training or background or effort. It wasn't something earned or cultivated, only received. There was no reason why this beauty had to exist. It simply *did*, as a matter of unqualified and unbidden gratuity, generating blessing to all within earshot. Somehow none of the trials he had gone through, including the self-inflicted ones, had been able to diminish the gift. Wilson was not only singing about the Big Relief; he was embodying it. This, I knew in my bones, was a thread worth following.

The presence of God is the only possible explanation for what I witnessed. Not just any god but the God of grace whose favor targets the undeserving, the Spirit whose "power is made perfect in weakness" (2 Cor. 12:9). The only deity I know who fits that description is named Jesus.

Wilson's song talks about love and mercy as something we *need*—now. Tomorrow will be too late. We need it tonight. The word *need* lends the chorus its immediacy. Religious people sometimes get nervous about placing too much emphasis on what they call "felt needs." The hesitancy is understandable. Anyone who's recently spent an afternoon with a teenager knows that feelings are not always trustworthy. They can be quite flimsy, fluctuating according to

3. Brian Wilson, "Love and Mercy," *Brian Wilson*, Warner Records Inc., 1988.

blood sugar and REM cycles. We should be cautious about believing something merely because it makes us feel better. This applies to the Big Relief of God's grace just as much as any other consolation we encounter in life.

But it would be callous to fault God for speaking the language of the heart. I for one would be far more suspicious of a God who didn't. We are, after all, affective creatures at bottom. If the gospel addresses us where we actually live, then its emotional traction is not secondary. A faith that provides no tangible relief would be thin gruel indeed, more of an intellectual exercise than something to give your whole life to.

The goal of *The Big Relief* has been to show the appeal and plausibility of grace in a world that wears us out with all sorts of escalating pressures.[4] My aim has been to make the grace of God not just spiritually or intellectually intelligible but emotionally so. And yet, grace is ultimately a relief because it is true, not the other way around. The same way we crave food because our bodies need it, we crave grace because it answers our real, objective spiritual predicaments: guilt, lack of love, death, separation from God. Our felt need is trustworthy—a corollary to our need for the God who personified it in his Son. Which is to say, our thirst for grace may wax and wane according to cultural conditions, but it is no social construct. Grace lies at the heart of the universe and is stamped into the fabric of creation. God's disposition runs gloriously rampant in the world.

One last dangling tension to mention: the Big Relief continually comes into conflict with attempts to domesticate it. Grace is such an unassailable good in the life of the world that we naturally try to harness and control it. The way this works in Christian settings is that we turn grace into a new law. We talk about those who "get it" and those who don't. We start to judge other Christians according to

---

4. There are, needless to say, plenty of other pressures that we contend with that I did not explore: the pressure to improve, the pressure to perform, the pressure to be good, the pressure to leave a legacy, the pressure to save the world, the pressure to say the right thing, etc. Some are more timely than others, but none are purely external in origin, which means that the dynamics of the Big Relief will find purchase there too.

how gracious they are—and condemn ourselves for our failures to be as grace-filled and forgiving as God is. In this way, as oxymoronic as it sounds (and is!), grace can become a new test of purity. I've seen it happen hundreds of times, an unfortunate by-product of the life-changing excitement and passion that the Big Relief so often inspires.

Fortunately, the Holy Spirit cannot be contained. The Spirit of God is always escaping the traps we set and returning us to dependence on the one who *is* gracious to misguided sinners of all persuasions. That includes those of us who co-opt the Big Relief for our own justification. While the fearful human proclivity toward mastery is something to be ever mindful of—especially in the church—not even that can sully the assurance Jesus provides. The grace of God has the final say. It is not bound by church walls and will outlast any institution that attempts to quell its fire.

In fact, to return to the burning building analogy in the introduction, the church may crumble down to the embers, but the God revealed in Jesus Christ has a knack for bringing life out of death. Things may look different than they have in the past, but wherever the church embraces its role as a dispensary of grace, delivering the goods week after week after week, life abounds. Communities that keep their focus vertical—that is, on the God who dispenses relief—invariably flourish. Those who understand their role differently tend to have a harder time.

Of course, no one gets it one hundred percent right. Not even Brian Wilson. None of us ever graduate from our need for the Big Relief. Thankfully, as the world wears itself out—as we wear *ourselves* out helping and hurting—there's one unchained melody that never ceases beckoning us to bask in its golden notes. It's the song broadcasting from on high that twists and turns and only grows more absorbing the closer you listen. The one about love and mercy and how the grace of God can, has, and will save the world. Starting, I pray, with you and with me.

DAVID ZAHL is the founder and director of Mockingbird Ministries, editor in chief of the *Mockingbird* blog, and cohost of the *Mockingcast* and *Brothers Zahl* podcasts. He is the author of *Seculosity: How Career, Parenting, Technology, Food, Politics, and Romance Became Our New Religion and What to Do about It* and *Low Anthropology: The Unlikely Key to a Gracious View of Others (and Yourself)*. He has also written for *Christianity Today* and the *Washington Post*. He and his family live in Charlottesville, Virginia, where he serves on the staff of Christ Episcopal Church.

Connect with David

 www.mbird.com  @mockingbirdnyc

 @mockingbirdmin  @mockingbirdmin